Low Whistle Makers Anthology

Daniel Bingamon

JUBILEE INSTRUMENTS & CRAFTS

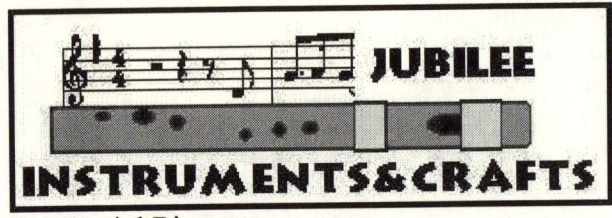

By: Daniel Bingamon
  Jubilee Music Instrument Co.
  1573 King Ave. BOX 227
  Kings Mills, OH 45034
  Phone: 513-398-8617
Web: www.bingamon.com/jubilee.htm

Cover - Jubilee Music Instrument Co. Logo and High whistle headjoint by Daniel Bingamon

Self-Published as "Low Whistle Makerss Anthology":
6th CreateSpace version – May 2015
5th Edition – 2012
4th Edition – January 2007
3rd Edition – June 2006
2nd Edition – 2005
First Edition – 2003
© 2003-2015 by Daniel Bingamon
Kings Mills, Ohio

Published as "Low Whistle Maker's Anthology":

Copyright © 2015 Daniel Bingamon
All rights reserved.
ISBN: 1512103209
ISBN-13: 978-1512103205

DEDICATION

I dedicate this book to my Wife, Anita, who has given me the time and encouragement to do this.

PREFACE

This book will take you through whistle physics, design and making. It contains construction hints, tricks, procedures and a table with one and a half octaves worth of plans for different tin/penny whistle keys. It gets into technical details as well as simple instructions; it is for the hobbyist and advanced maker as well.

I hope you enjoy this book and have hours of fun with instruments that you can build yourself.
Daniel Bingamon
Written: November 2002

Bingamon's Tin Whistle Builders Anthology

CONTENTS:

Introduction

Chapter 1: Tin Whistle Anatomy
  The Parts, How does it tick?
  Types of Tin Whistles

Chapter 2: The Bore
  Frequency, Temperature, Speed of Sound, L/B Ratio, W/B Ratio, Materials

Chapter 3: The Toneholes
  Formulas, Cut off Frequency, Effects on size, Undercutting, Adding Keys

Chapter 4: The Fipple
  Fipple Parts, The Windsheet, The Windway and its dimensions, The Floor,
  The Roof, The Edge, The Block, Chamfering, The Beak
  Testing Techniques:
    The Frozen Fipple Test (Lips beware)
    Water Flow Test
    Stick in the Fipple Test
    Organ Pipe Ears

Chapter 5: Tuning
    Build a tunable instrument - please

Chapter 6: Being Aware of End User Desires
  Playing Techniques, Fingering Styles (pipers fingering)

Chapter 7: Problems

Water Clogged Instruments, Using Dupanol and other anti-clogging agents,
Alternative Methods, 2nd Register pitch, Weakness between registers,
Hiss or "Airy" sound

Chapter 8: Materials
Kinds and Grades of materials, Impact of using certain materials,
Mixing different Materials, Glues

Chapter 9: Tools (and proper use)

Appendix

Frequency Tables, Scales of all kinds, Instrument measurement Tables
Whistle Assembly Pictorial, Suppliers, Index

Introduction

Back in the middle 1990's, I took up playing Recorder. Though I had played before when I was younger (in School), I had an interest in playing it whenever I went on a business trip. After all, they can kick you out of a hotel from playing a trumpet but a Recorder is not very loud.
What I found out about Recorders, it seems the Recorder players play only music of musicians that have long passed away. I'm little more interested in a bit more modern music. During this quest, two things happened. One, my interest in making instruments had fired up again. Two, the Tin whistle (or Pennywhistle), a folk instrument - you can play anything that you want on it. You're not connected with a certain form of music. Although the Tin Whistle is associated with Celtic music, it can be applied to anything else as well.

I've had a desire to teach for some time and was a staff member of the MIMF.COM a few years ago. (Music Instrument Makers Forum, Wind Instruments Section)
It's only fitting that I put my collection of information in the form of a small book.

CHAPTER ONE: Tin Whistle Anatomy

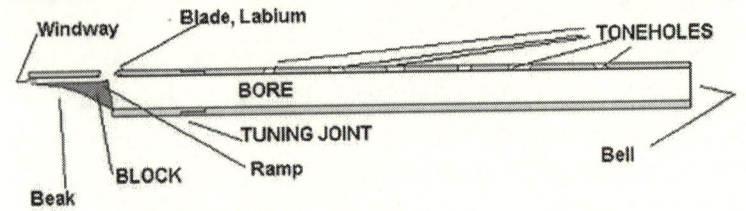

[Diagram of a tin whistle with labels: Windway, Blade/Labium, Toneholes, Bore, Tuning Joint, Bell, Ramp, Block, Beak]

The whistle diagram pictured above uses the traditional ramped block method to deliver air across the labium. Other methods keep the windway above the blade line. This will be discussed later.

Note the small ramp where the block approaches the labium, whistles designed this way are critically influenced by the accuracy of this ramp.

Types of Tin Whistles

Types of Tin Whistles can be identified by the various types of materials and construction techniques. I have defined these below:

MATERIAL

Tin Whistles at one time were actually made of rolled up Tin sheets. Starting out with Clarks Pennywhistles, nearly a hundred years ago. The blocks used to be made of lead – not recommended.
Today, Tin Whistles are made of Wood, Plastics, PVC, Aluminum, Copper, Nickel-Silver, Brass, Stainless Steel and nearly any other material conceivable.
So first, we have the material as a classification. This is simple part. From here is gets more complicated.

DIMENSIONAL CHARACTERISTICS

Material has some effect on the sound of an instrument, however - it is the dimensional characteristic afforded by the material that has a greater impact on sound.
Take wood for example, wood has to be thicker for structural integrity. Because of this, the bore is thicker and the toneholes have deeper chimneys. (The Chimney is the area in-between the bore and the surface of the instrument.)

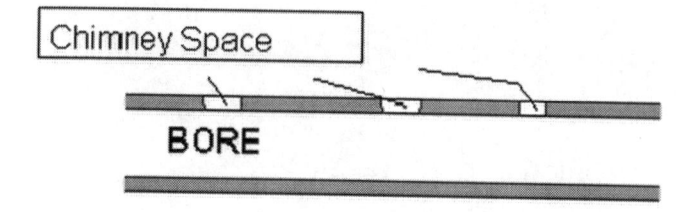

CHAPTER TWO: The Bore

CYLINDRICAL and CONICAL BORES

The bore is the hollow tube that makes up the main shape of the instrument.
Tin Whistles can have Cylindrical or Conical Bores

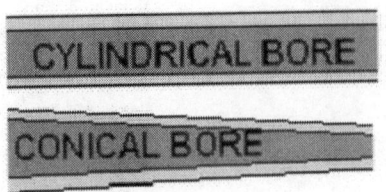

CYLINDRICAL BORE

CONICAL BORE

The Cylindrical Bore is easier to make whereas the Conical Bore allows the finger spacing to be closer together.

Cylindrical bores are convenient to the builders for a great number of reasons.
1. The formulas for calculating hole positions is easier.
2. You can obtain cylindrical tubes easily to produce instruments.
3. You do not have to invest in expensive tapers or special metal forming equipment.

Conical bores are usually wide near the mouthpiece and reduce in diameter as you go down. Because the bore diameter reduces in size, it has some affect on the vibrating column of air that brings the toneholes closer together which works well for small finger spacing.

A bore does not have to be round. There are a few Recorders made with square bores, organ pipes can have square bores. Small tin whistles can be built from square brass tubing stock. In fact, square brass whistles have a very comfortable feel but it's hard to find the tone holes on a flat surface.

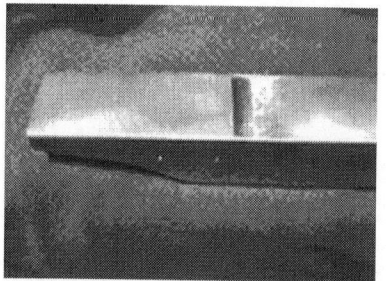

A Square whistle mouthpiece

Frequency

The base frequency of a Tin Whistle bore is based on the length of the bore. Other factors have an effect on the frequency. The speed of sound is a important component of determining the Tin Whistles base frequency.
The speed of sound is between 700 and 800 miles per hour. It changes with temperature, this is why whistles go out of tune when they vary in temperature.
Standard tuning of whistles is performed at 73 degrees Fahrenheit

The formulas here are metric, conversions will be provided, here is how it works.

Speed of sound = (20.06 * sqrt(273.0 + Celsius temperature)

The sqrt() is the abbreviation for a Square Root function.

Many designers use 73 Deg. F or 22.8 Deg C for the temperature.

Once the speed of sound is determined in meters per second, we can determine how long that our bore tube needs to be.

First, we need the wavelength: (units in Centimeters)

Wavelength = (Speed of Sound * 100) / Desired Frequency

The Wavelength is divided in half to determine the theoretical tube length.

Theoretical Length = Wavelength / 2

Also called "Nominal Length", expressed as:

Nom Length = Speed of Sound (cm/sec) / Frequency / 2

Now there is a small problem, the air traveling through the tube actually travels beyond the tube until the stream breaks up. But this value can be determined by math.

Real Length = Theoretical Length − (0.6133 * End of Bore Diameter / 2)
We use 'End of Bore Diameter' because with a conical whistle, the bore will be a different diameter on the other end.

This is called, "End Correction".
Additional formulas are applied to set the position of the fipple hole.
In addition to this, we have the L/B or Length / Bore Ratio. The L/B Ratio deals with the proper tubing diameter that goes with a whistle.
It's actually pretty flexible, the ratio for a tinwhistle is usually between 20 and 34, a value of about 24 to 26 though is usually ideal for tinwhistle design.
The L/B ratio on conical whistles is measured using the upper part of the whistle where the diameter is the largest. The L/B ratio for cylindrical whistles uses the 'average' bore diameter. A more scientific version of the L/B ratio is the Wavelength-to-Bore ratio. This ratio is more scientific because the math is not affected by the End Correction

Materials

Tin Whistles can be made from numerous materials, the thickness of these materials in the bore will affect the sound of a whistle.

> Copper, Aluminum or Brass pipe: A bright sound, rich in harmonics with quick response.

> Wood, PVC pipe, Bamboo: Thicker material gives a mellow, sometimes sweet `sound with limited response.

Some materials allow vibrations to emanate through the walls and this has some effect on the sound, however the dimensions afforded by various materials yield the greatest impact. Metal sounds bright because of its thinness, note that plastic and wood have some similarities because they usually have similar thicknesses.

FIPPLE CHARACTERISTICS

The form of the fipple, whether it is a square hole or rectangular will have an effect of the sound. A more 'squarish' hole will sound "flutey" whereas a rectangular hole can sound "reedy" depending on the distance across the hole and the width.

CHAPTER THREE: The Toneholes

The toneholes are the holes being covered by your fingers

A tonehole of a certain diameter in a certain place will play the right note, the same tonehole can be made smaller and moved up higher and play the same note. You can enlarge the tonehole in a lower position and still play the correct note. In all cases, the note may be perfectly in tune but a few problems crop up. If the tonehole gets too small, it will sound weak and muffled, maybe not even sound at all. Fortunately, we have math on our side to help predict the toneholes performance

So let's explore the formulas for calculating tonehole positions:

First we must decide on a diameter for our drill size. For Low Whistles, 3/8" is probably a good starting point and then make adjustments as needed to make it comfortably fit our hands. For High Whistles, maybe ¼" drill as a starter.

You will need to know the frequencies of each tonehole and the base frequency (the frequency of all holes closed). For Low-D, here are the frequencies:

D=293.660, E=329.622, F#=369.988, G=391.989, A=439.993, B=493.875, C#=554.356,

So there you have it, the base frequency and the frequency of six toneholes.
Now, earlier I mentioned the length/bore ratio. Assuming that you have found material to meet this ratio, we need a bore diameter and the thickness of the wall.

In this example, I'm going to use PVC pipe – Schedule 40 grade. This brand has an inner diameter of 0.824 inches and 0.113 inch thickness.

The formula for calculating toneholes uses the metric system, that makes the bore diameter 2.093 centimeters and the thickness as 0.287 cm.

By the way, Benade's equations refer to bore diameter as '2a' and hole diameter as '2b'.

All the calculations below will be in metric units unless otherwise stated:

For this calculation, I'm going to introduce a constant, 34500 as the speed of sound.

The toneholes must be calculated from lowest frequency to highest frequency.

The first thing we must do is to calculate starting variables for the base frequency.

    1. Calculate theoretical length by (speed of sound / base frequency / 2)
        Answer: 34500/ 293.660 / 2 = 58.741

    2. Calculate End Hole Correction by (0.6133 * bore diameter / 2)
        Answer: 0.6133 * 2.093 / 2) = 0.6418

    3. Calculate Music Length by (Theoretical length – End Hole Correction)
        Answer: 58.741 – 0.6418 = 58.0705

Now the actual instrument will be smaller and this will depend on the size of the fipple hole, we'll get to that later.

The next step is to sequentially calculate each tonehole. But there is a problem, the formula requires us to do each tonehole from bottom up. The area of covered toneholes above that tonehole affects the lower tonehole that we are working on. Until those holes are calculated, that information will be unknown. Therefore, these tonehole formulas are "iterative". This means that we have to recalculate everything over again after we find out more information. The more times that we recalculate, the more accurate the estimation becomes.

Since the next note is E, I will use it for the example.

Here is the sequence for calculating toneholes.

1. Calculate a value called "Chimney height" by taking
(wall thickness + (hole diameter x 0.75))
The official variable name for this is called 'TE', we'll refer to it as chimney height.   A hole diameter of 15/64, 0.234" or 0.595 cm

    Calculate: 0.287 + (0.595 * 0.75)

    Answer for the E note: 0.7335

2. Next, calculate theoretical length or 'nominal length (L)' by
(Speed of sound / frequency / 2)

    Calculate: 34500/ 329.622 / 2

    Answer for the E note: 52.333

3. Calculate 'hole spacing' also called '2S' by (previous holes length – Theoretical length)
   If this is the bottommost hole, compare it to the base frequencies theoretical length.

   Calculate: <u>58.741 - 52.333</u>

   <u>Answer for the E note: 6.409</u>

4. And now, the complicated one, 'Local Cutoff Frequency' also called 'fc'.
   Take (Speed of sound x hole diameter / bore diameter / 2 / pi / √(chimney height x hole spacing)

   Calculate: <u>34500 * 0.595 / 2.093 / 2 / 3.141593 / sqrt(0.7335 * 6.409)</u>

   <u>Answer for the E note: 720.335</u>

5. Calculate Open hole Correction
   Now here there is a bit of complication. The first toneholes formula is different than the others.

   First tonehole formula:

   Effective Chimney height / ((hole diameter / bore diameter) to the 2nd power + effective chimney height x (1 / hole spacing))

   Note ^x symbol means raise to the power of x.

   Calculate: <u>0.7335 / ((0.595 / 2.093)^2 + 0.7335 * (1 / 6.409))</u>

Answer: 3.7547

Second and other toneholes formulas:

Hole spacing x 0.5 * (sqrt (1 + 4 x eff chimney height / hole spacing x (bore diameter / hole diameter) to the 2nd power) − 1)

Answer: 5.0644 if you would have used the other formula

6. Calculate 'New Hole Positions'
   Take Theoretical length − Open Hole Correction

   Answer: 48.578

Well, now you have it.
The next iteration, you recalculate everything except that the hole spacing '2s' is calculated based on the 'New Hole Positions' of the previous iteration instead of using the 'Theoretical or Nominal Length'.

Run it about 5 times, and you should have something pretty accurate.

Or, skip all this and download my TWCALC (Tin Whistle Calculator) from the internet. You can download this from my website.

Local Cutoff Frequency

Local Cutoff Frequency deals with

Another very important physical quantity is the "cutoff frequency" fc.
This marks the boundary between low frequencies, which are reflected
by the tone holes back into the instrument to form strong resonances,
and high frequencies which leak freely out through the tone hole row.
The cutoff frequency also marks the division between the low-frequency
isotropic radiation pattern (energy radiates in all directions equally)

Effects on Size

Tone holes can be moved to a lower position but in order to continue playing the same frequency the hole must be enlarged. To move the hole to a higher position, the hole will have to get smaller in diameter. A tradeoff of moving a hole higher up to get closer to the other holes is that the hole can speak weaker. This weaker sound can be predicted in the design phase by checking the 'Local Cutoff Frequency'. Typically, the local cutoff frequency of a tonehole needs to be more than twice the toneholes actual frequency.

Undercutting

Toneholes can be increased in diameter without actually increasing the diameter by a process known as undercutting. When air flows across through a hole, it does not use the entire area of the hole. Certain turbulences develop due to the geometery of the hole – at this point we get into fluid dynamics. Certain shapes tend to allow the air to use the hole more efficiently.

Here, a chart that shows 'pipe loss coefficients'. Note, the last hole in this chart shows the most efficient type of hole.

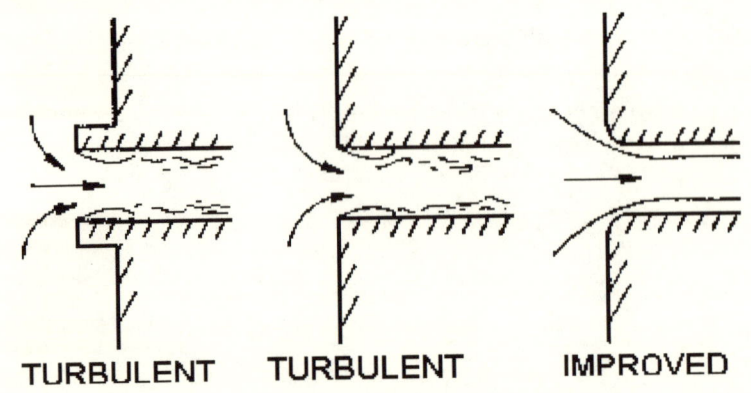

TURBULENT   TURBULENT   IMPROVED

Lower efficiency holes pose a problem on various octaves. Given the fact that air rides closer to the surface as pressure increases, a hole that is inefficient and cause pretend to open up more in the upper octave. A well undercut hole that has high efficiency does not allow for this to happen.
Note that the third example as some round on the edges.

For example, say a certain tonehole with sharp edges is only 65% efficient. As the pressure increases, let's say the efficiency increase 10%. Now we're at 75%.

If a tonehole is 95% efficient, the area of the hole cannot increase by 10% because the air efficiency can never exceed 100%. It is the limit to the physical area.

A toneholes efficiency is the ratio of the area the air sees versus the physical area of the hole. There is equipment to measure this, but it is very expensive.

Adding Keys

Sometimes, the person playing has small hands or you need to make a whistle in an unusually low key. Adding the use keys will make the instrument playable.

To replace a normal tonehole, requires a normally open key, there are many ways to do this.

Here is the side view of a normally open key.

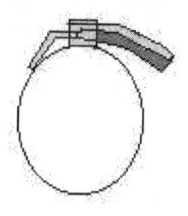

A normally open key needs to have a lever that is hinged with the pad covering the tonehole. A spring is employed to key to keep the key from flopping loose and sets the open position above the tonehole. Now this is important, the tonehole will be influenced by the key hovering over it, you either must oversize the hole like they do on Boehm style concert flutes or make the pad high enough to not influence the hole. Typically in folk instruments, we do a little bit of both. The key being slightly high and causing interference when moved into place can be a good thing. The allows the player to use the key to bend notes and ornament in the traditional Irish music as well as many other folk music styles.

A simple normally open key can be made with pivot screws and needle springs, obtained from Ferree's Music Instrument tools in Michigan (800-253-2261)..

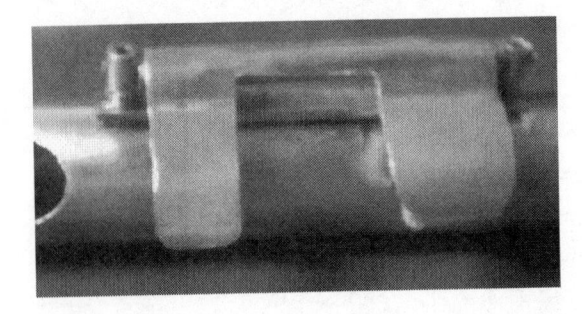

The key in the above picture is made to operate like the normally open keys on a Clarinet or Flute. It can be easily cut out of brass stock using a $10.00 Radio Shack Nibbling Tool. The hard part is drilling the 0.032 hole for the needle spring. You might be able to pickup a junk clarinet or flute from Ebay and use the parts.

To make it easier for the hobbyist, I designed a normally open key that uses a coil spring.

The spring is located under the lever. The little solder mark in the middle of it is a tiny brass nail soldered in place and then cut short to make a spring retainer. A similar thing is done on the body of the whistle only upside down (nail head soldered to body).

In the back is a little tab that keeps the key from over opening. You're currently seeing it in the closed position.

For long keys, a string could be used to link the lever mechanism to the pad mechanism.
The example below uses thick PVC pipe for a good mounting surface.

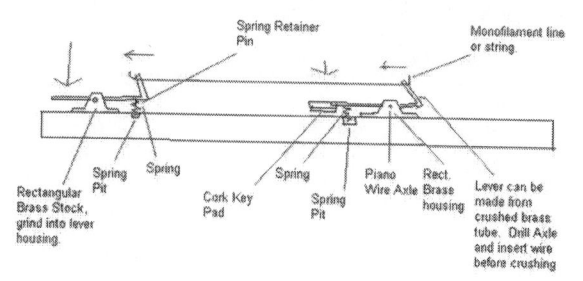

When I developed the first bass whistle, I used double acting lever keys.

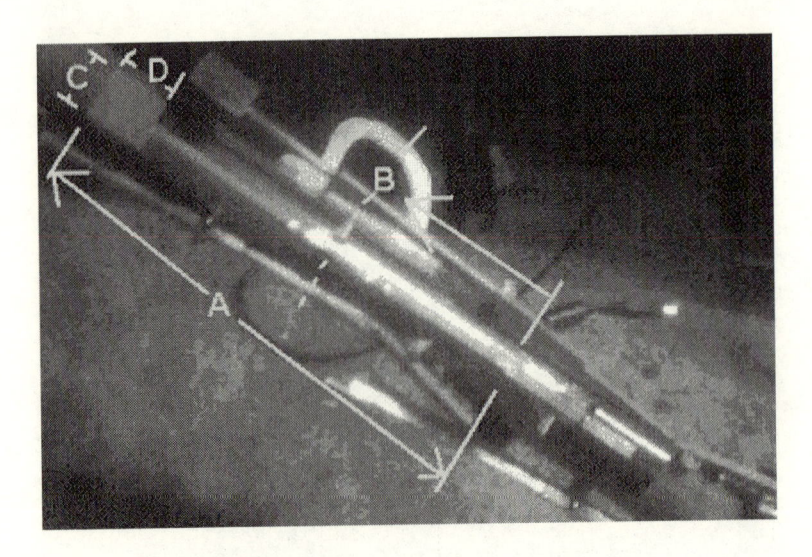

In the later models, I used a pivoting rod system.

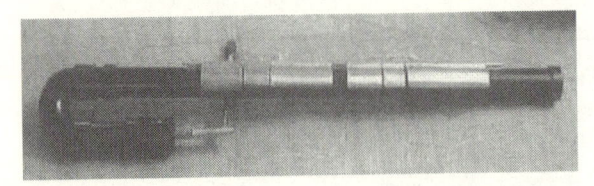

Some time ago, I wrote up a web page on making normally closed keys, here is that information:

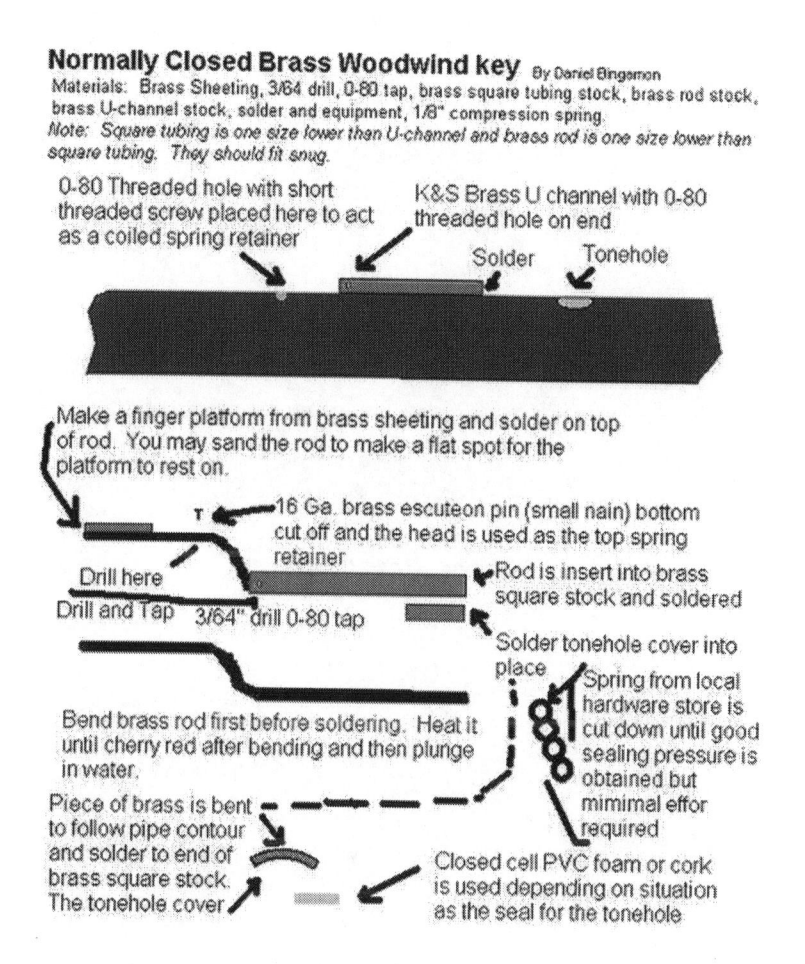

Normally Closed Brass Woodwind key By Daniel Bingamon

Materials: Brass Sheeting, 3/64 drill, 0-80 tap, brass square tubing stock, brass rod stock, brass U-channel stock, solder and equipment, 1/8" compression spring.
Note: Square tubing is one size lower than U-channel and brass rod is one size lower than square tubing. They should fit snug.

0-80 Threaded hole with short threaded screw placed here to act as a coiled spring retainer

K&S Brass U channel with 0-80 threaded hole on end

Solder   Tonehole

Make a finger platform from brass sheeting and solder on top of rod. You may sand the rod to make a flat spot for the platform to rest on.

16 Ga. brass escuteon pin (small nain) bottom cut off and the head is used as the top spring retainer

Drill here

Drill and Tap   3/64" drill 0-80 tap

Rod is insert into brass square stock and soldered

Solder tonehole cover into place

Spring from local hardware store is cut down until good sealing pressure is obtained but mimimal effor required

Bend brass rod first before soldering. Heat it until cherry red after bending and then plunge in water.

Piece of brass is bent to follow pipe contour and solder to end of brass square stock. The tonehole cover.

Closed cell PVC foam or cork is used depending on situation as the seal for the tonehole

Note, the process of heat the rod after bending is called annealing. Brass will work harden after you bend it, heat it, drill. You have to anneal it once in a while or it will break or crack while working with it. After soldering, let it air cool instead of plunging and it will harden instead of being soft and bendable. This is called heat treating.

Leaf springs instead of coil springs can be purchased from Ferree's Music Instrument supply.

26

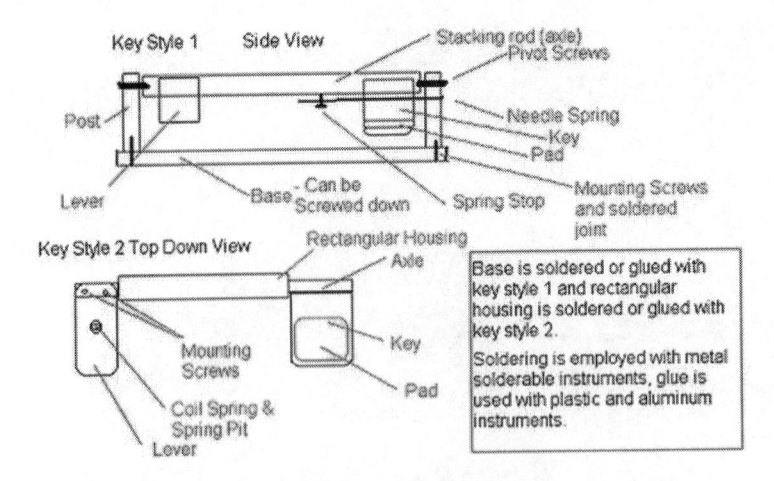

Here is a simple normally open key. The needle springs and pivot screws are obtained from Ferrees Tools.

FIPPLE TERMINOLOGY

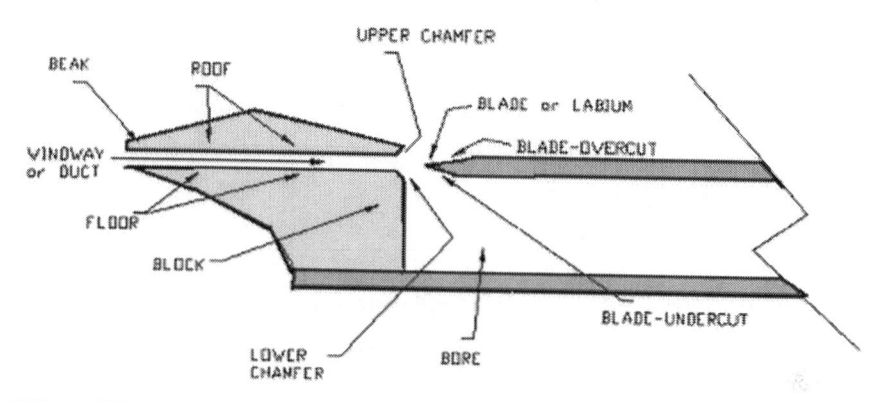

Diagram labels: BEAK, ROOF, UPPER CHAMFER, BLADE or LABIUM, BLADE-OVERCUT, WINDWAY or DUCT, FLOOR, BLOCK, LOWER CHAMFER, BORE, BLADE-UNDERCUT

The Fipple, Beak, Windway, Floor, Block:

As the whistle player places his/her lips over the beak and begins to play the whistle a number of things can happen.

The wind, traveling down the windway becomes focused and straightened. The windway may have an uphill or downhill ramp in its design. It might be curved, straight, D-shaped. Maybe it starts out wide and narrows. All of these factors affect the performance of the instrument. There are so many ways to design a fipple and a good number of these designs perform well. Obstructions, scratches, hanging slivers of plastic can interrupt the performance of this windway.

You might have the perfect windway acoustically speaking, but then you have to deal with human breath. Too long or narrow, it clogs with moisture. As a whistle designer, you have to fight with the perfect design demanded by physics and then you have to fight with mother nature who decides to give us moist breath.

Windsheet:

What the windway delivers is that very important sheet of air know as the 'windsheet'.

The 'Windsheet' is a three dimensional sheet of air that expels from the windway and pours across the fipples opening (known as the 'window'). This sheet starts by flowing over the 'blade' or 'labium'. The trajectory of this 'windsheet' is set by the height of the 'floor' of the windway, the position of the labium, the general angle of the windway and the chamfers.

Edges, Chamfers:

The chamfers are small angles cut in the block and the edge of the windway's roof. These are absolutely required to help the windsheet expand properly. The windsheet also changes in size depending on the pressure that you deliver. You can expect the windsheet to widen when you play in the second octave.

Testing Techniques

The Frozen Fipple Test:

This test, for most part works on whistles with metal fipples. It sometimes works on dark shiny plastic surfaces but not as well as metal. Put the whistle in fridge. After a few minutes of cooling, take it out and blow air into it a watch the vapor trail leave a foggy surface on the fipple. If your windway is irregular, the plume deposited on the surface will spill to one side instead of a nice symmetrical output. Don't get it too cold with lips stuck to the instrument.

The Water Flow Test

Taping the beak of the whistle to a water hose or faucet with duct tape. S-l-o-w-l-y turn on the water, not too much. You can watch a sheet of water come out the windway and flow across the labium (sharp edge). If the water flows to one side or the other, the whistle definitely has issues.

Stick in the Fipple Test

This is one of my favorite tests, you can use this to tweak very inexpensive whistles to sound very nicely. By moving the stick around in the windway, you'll find 'dead spots'. 'Dead spots' are areas where you can put the stick into and nothing changes, it's like the stick isn't even there – what that means to you is that this part of the fipple is not doing anything.

Once you find this dead spot, you need to modify the windway to encourage the airstream to use this space. A coffee stirring straw works the best.

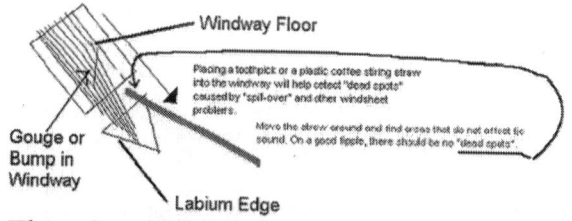

Windway Floor

Placing a toothpick or a plastic coffee stirring straw into the windway will help detect "dead spots" caused by "spill-over" and other windsheet problems.

Move the straw around and find areas that do not affect the sound. On a good fipple, there should be no "dead spots".

Gouge or Bump in Windway

Labium Edge

This also detects uneven labium edges. Note: the thin lines represent airflow.

Building a Water Trap

A water trap can be built into a whistle by have two blocks in the mouthpiece with a large cavity in-between. A water trap can catch moisture particulate, some have actually tried putting sponge-like material into the trap. It does not solve the problems of condensation but it is good for players who have problems with salivation.

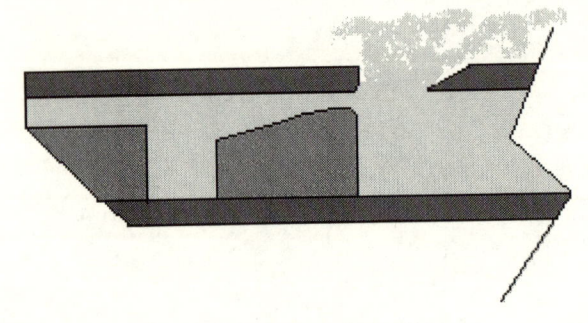

(Light blue represents airflow)

Water Trap Depiction (light blue represents air)
Water traps have been used one very large fipple flutes.

Organ Ears

Organ Ears are usually a U-shape that bends around the fipple opening or sometimes a thick material for the headjoint is used. If you have ever noticed, the fipple on Recorders are deep into the headjoint, the material around it causes the effect of 'Organ Ears'.
The term 'Organ Ears' come from Pipe Organs, this process was first used on pipe organs.

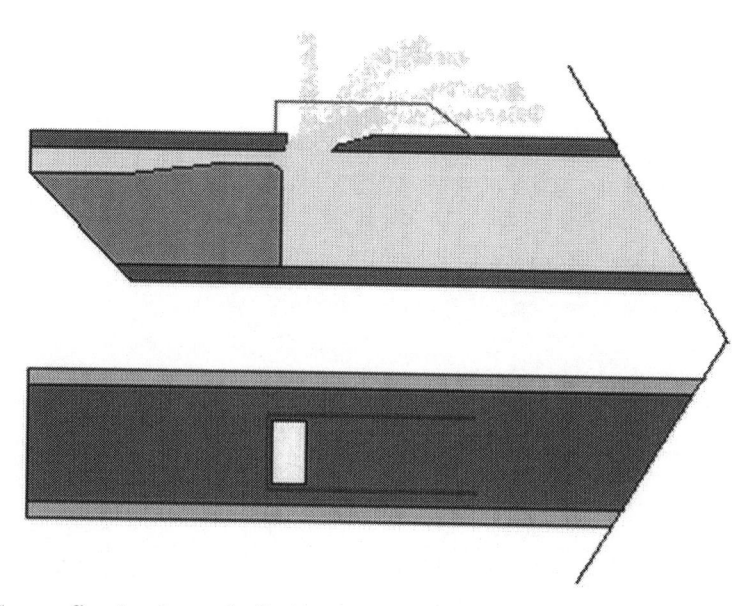

Some fipples have built in Organ Ears by building the beak cover all around the fipple.

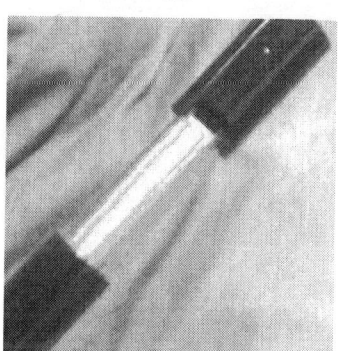

Tuning

Build tunable instrument, please:
Tin Whistles are sensitive to temperature change, a few degrees of temperature and you're out of tune. Lets look at the situation:

Tuning deviations from A440 Standard by Temperature Change

The Equally Tempered Scaled in A=440

Note Designation

Freq.(Hz) @70 Deg F

Deg F	70	Wavelength	65	70	75	80
Deg C	21.111	in cm	18.333	21.111	23.889	26.667
A3	220	156.414	218.959	220	221.036	222.067
A#3	233.082	147.635	231.979	233.082	234.179	235.272
B3	246.942	139.349	245.773	246.942	248.104	249.262
C4	261.626	131.528	260.388	261.626	262.858	264.084
C#4	277.183	124.146	275.871	277.183	278.488	279.787
D4	293.665	117.178	292.275	293.665	295.048	296.424
D#4	311.127	110.601	309.655	311.127	312.592	314.05
E4	329.628	104.394	328.068	329.628	331.18	332.725
F4	349.228	98.534	347.576	349.228	350.873	352.509
F#4	369.994	93.004	368.244	369.994	371.737	373.471
G4	391.995	87.784	390.141	391.995	393.841	395.679
G#4	415.305	82.857	413.34	415.305	417.26	419.207
A4	440	78.207	437.918	440	442.072	444.134
A#4	466.164	73.817	463.958	466.164	468.359	470.544
B4	493.883	69.674	491.547	493.883	496.209	498.524
C5	523.251	65.764	520.776	523.251	525.715	528.167
C#5	554.365	62.073	551.743	554.365	556.976	559.574
D5	587.33	58.589	584.551	587.33	590.095	592.848
D#5	622.254	55.301	619.31	622.254	625.184	628.1
E5	659.255	52.197	656.136	659.255	662.359	665.449
F5	698.456	49.267	695.152	698.456	701.745	705.019
F#5	739.989	46.502	736.488	739.989	743.473	746.942

G5	783.991	43.892	780.282	783.991	787.683	791.357
G#5	830.609	41.429	826.68	830.609	834.521	838.414
A5	880	39.103	875.837	880	884.144	888.268

% Error:	0.475	0	-0.469	-0.931

Given this chart, we can see that a High-D whistle tuned at 70 degrees F, will produce 587.33 Hz, now we take that whistle outdoors in the summer to 80 Degrees, and it now puts out 592.848 Hz. That's almost 16 cents sharp on a tuner.

Incidently, 100 cents on a tuner is amout of space between two notes. So from 587.33 (High-D) to 622.254 (High-D#) is 100 cents, half-way or 50 cents is 604.792 Hz..

Now there are other factors involved here. Typically, instruments are designed so that they are in perfect tune at 70 Deg F. This does not mean that you use 70 Deg. F in your tonehole equations, typically a designer will use 80-85 degrees for high whistle and 70-80 for low whistles. Remember, human breath is 98.6 Deg. F. When it goes into a metal or plastic whistle it cools some. Also, a whistle needs to be warmed up by playing before tuning is to take place.

Remember that warm hands also influences the whistles tuning, some people have cold hands and yes this has a little bit of influence on tuning. So please make your instruments tuneable.

Being Aware of End User Desires

Playing Techniques

Musicians are fussy people, there are no two alike. Some have good habits, bad habits or just different habits (not necessarily good or bad). In Tin Whistles, we have our share of problems.

Here are a few to name:

One person says, "whistle is in tune" another person says "it's not in tune".

People get used to a certain brand of whistles. The person playing a scale starts at the bottom of the whistle and proceeds up the scale giving a certain amount of air to each note. Now, another whistle player will go up the scale and deliver more or less air to each note. Sometime the player will give more air to the higher notes of the scale, the whistle goes out of tune. It is not necessarily a bad whistle. If fact, most whistles are not designed to be in tune at maximum air velocity. This would make a poor instrument since the 'F' note on a 'D' whistle would thus be soft and the 'B' note would be very loud. This would drive a recording artist crazy. You want a whistle to have as uniform of a volume level as it will let you on that first octave. The second octave is going to be louder, hopefully we strive to keep it from getting terribly louder. Some Irish Flutes are actually flat on the low notes so that the user can blow harder and make them sharpen into tune with more volume.

Some players want an 'airy' sound, others want a 'pure' sound.

There are probably more players that want the 'pure' nowdays.

'Flutey' sound or 'Reedy' sound?
Once again, this is a player's desire. If would be good to describe what your instrument sounds like to potential buyers or have 'WAV' files online.

Also remember, you can't please everyone.

Fingering Styles (piper's fingering)

Several years ago, pipers fingering was introduced for Low Whistles. If you're building an instrument that is likely to be played with piper's fingering, make sure that they play it that way. Some of us prefer 'fingertip fingering' instead of 'piper's fingering'.

Problems

Water Clogged Instruments

Tin Whistles are subject to being clogged in the windway by breath moisture or saliva.

Breath generated moisture being the most common, as a whistle warms up it will clog less often. Metal instruments will no doubtedly clog more often because the tone body will cool more to room temperature.

Construction techniques can be applied to the windway to help prevent clogging.
Mainly, reducing the length of the windway helps – but the tradeoff is that the windsheet is more turbulent. The trick is to get the length short enough to not affect the performance and not clog as easy. The height of the windway is a major factor, but this can be easily resolved by making the windway tapered (spike shaped). Wide inlet at the lips and narrowing.

Using Dupanol and other anti-clogging agents

Dupanol, is a soap and water mixture that is soaked in a piece of paper and then the windway is treated with this mixture and it is set out to dry. It helps disperse water

droplets and will last a few sessions. It is best not to ship instruments with this form of
treatment added, people will most likely complain that the instrument worked fine when
they first bought it and then it started clogging. Another potential complaint is that the
instrument tastes like soap. Let the end user do the treating.
Don't use Rain-X or Jet Dri – don't recommend it, this stuff can by poisonous in large
Quantities.

Alternative Methods

Some people have reported making a foam air filter to catch moisture, I haven't heard any positive results on this to date.

A company by the name of "Smallparts" sells a porous plastic material, it would be Interesting to attempt to use this in a windway.

2nd Register pitch
Sometimes tuning between the first and second octaves can be inconstant. Maybe the second register goes flat. Here are some facts to remember, the second register has a slightly higher air pressure in the bore. High frequency tends to bounce off the walls a little differently. You find the porous nature of the bore, small holes, crevices,

all of this is noticed more by high frequency. Therefore, increased area noticed by the high frequency makes the upper octave play flat.
Flutes, use a taper in the body or in the head to help alleviate this problem.

Weakness between registers

Notes in the second octave are produced by higher pressure, more air means more volume. You can't get a perfect consistency of volume level between the two octaves. Ways to resolve this can be done by venting the bore at the point where the high pressure node is supposed to occur. On Tin whistle, this would require sometime that is unacceptable – a register hole or thumb hole. To avoid this, the top tonehole is design to be close to the half-way length position and the user is instructed to slightly vent that top hole. It will cause the pressure to drop and encourage the second octave to form with less air delivered.

Hiss or "Airy" sound

This is a difficult problem to resolve in whistle making because there are many things that can cause this.

The first thing is the aiming of the windsheet. The 'windsheet' must exit the windway, cross over the hole and run across the sharp edge.

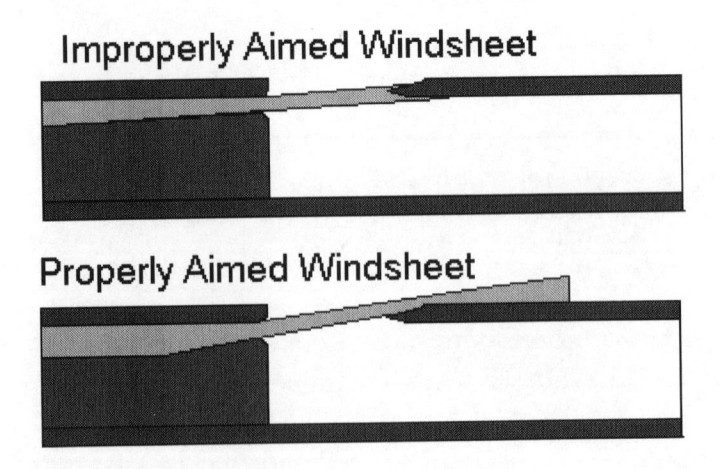

Improperly Aimed Windsheet

Properly Aimed Windsheet

The above illustration uses the in-pipe notched block windway. The desire here is to get the windsheet to flow close to sharp edge (labium). If the edge is too sharp, it will produce a low volume whistling at an undesired frequency. Also in this example, the improperly aimed windsheet is flowing air directly into the bore, this direct air makes the instrument weak sounding and 'airy' sounding.

Aiming the Windsheet is not our only problem, making the cut in the blade is important as well. In the next illustration, we have a shrouded windway design with a improperly cut labium and an improperly cut labium. A major mistake of first-time whistle builder is that they file down a nice blade on the surface of the labium and they fail to cut the underside. The example below though is underside that was undercut too much. In this case, much air spills into the bore making the first register weak and a very air bore sound. Note that the properly cut blade does allow a very small amount of leakage of the air stream into the bore. This is good to have if it is very-very slight, it encourages the intitial surge of air to go into oscillation immediately.

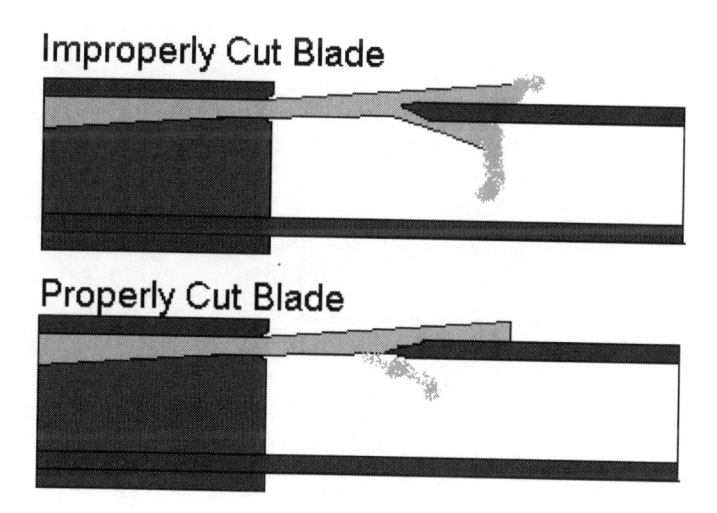

Improperly Cut Blade

Properly Cut Blade

A gouge in the windway can deflect the airstream to where is totally misses the blade even when peering down the windway says that the whistle should operate.

In this case, blowing hard enough on the whistle may coax some of the wind into the bore to get it to sound. If this example happens to work, it is likely to produce a lot of 'chiff'. Chiff is the sound produced on the initial startup of sound or oscillation. In this case the large amount of 'chiff' is the whistle trying to start up.

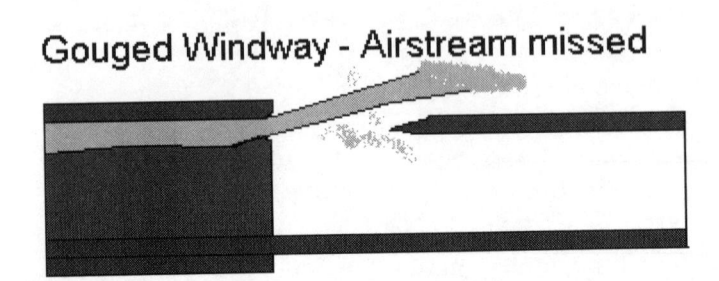

Gouged Windway - Airstream missed

The windsheet is formed by shape of the windway, remember that it changes dimensions in the upper register – the whistle design must accommodate this. Some whistles will buzz slightly on certain notes because of improper 'voicing' of the fipple.

If you were building the shrouded windway design, this design uses the thickness of the metal to make the height of the windway. What if the windway isn't tall enough, what if the sharp edge is too thin to profile? Telescoping tubing can be used in some cases to double the thickness of the wall. You will find this technique used on many brass custom-made high whistles. Make sure to carefully test the tuning on higher notes on the whistle, the area change here can affect their pitch.

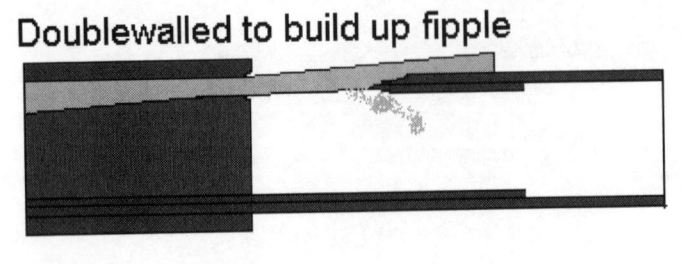

Doublewalled to build up fipple

Materials

Kinds and Grades of materials

Stainless Steel
> Stainless steel is a bit on the heavy side for whistlemaking. Too heavy for high whistle but possibly good for low whistle. Material galls easy when cutting and drilling. Peck drilling could be employed (drill a little and back out repeatedly - spray with WD40 or some coolant)
> It is absolutely necessary to have the drill speed just right when drilling. A very shiny finish can be obtained and it is low maintenance. Silver solder can be used with it.
> You can find this through Smallparts.

Nickel Silver
> Nickel-Silver also called German-Silver doesn't actually have silver in it. It used by the major concert flute manufactures and keeps it shine for a long time. It drills similar to brass and is solderable with ordinary solders or Braze. Bagpipe builders use it for ferrules and keys on Northumbrian pipes.
> Treat similar to hard brass. It makes a beautiful sound. You can obtain this through Copper and Brass Sales Co. and some Jewelry equip. suppliers.

Brass

Brass keeps much better than copper however it also oxidizes by developing a patina (darkening of color from oxidation). Brass music instruments are usually covered with a lacquer finish. Drill speed needs to be set accurately while drilling toneholes. Center drilling End Mills are a good way to drill brass. It has been said that when drilling brass, don't use the drill on anything else. It is solderable with ordinary solders. Typically sounds better than copper. A good suppler is www.specialshapes.com or Hobbytown stores.

Copper

Copper drills nicely, it discolors easily and should be clear coated or painted.
I've tried copper blackening and browning chemical but they chip easily and do not produce a very uniform finish. Solderable with ordinary plumbing solder. Copper polishes well but requires coating immediately afterwards. Wire brushing also produces attractive results.

Type M is the general thin wall and makes good tonebodies, type L is a little heavier and makes good fipples. You can find it at most hardware stores.

Aluminum

A number of whistles are made of Aluminum, fastening is usually performed by gluing or rivets. Aluminum can welded with special equipment. Drilling is easy. Typically thicker walls are used compared to brass or copper for more strength. EMT tubing though Electronic Supplies is a good way to find aluminum. Some farm supply stores have unusual sizes. Also try specialshapes.com

Tin

Tin Whistles were originally made from Tin, it is solderable. It requires protective coating such as paint. Tin cannot be found in tubing form, you have to roll it solder it yourself. Can be found in sheet form at most hardware stores in heating equipment departments.

PVC

PVC – Polyvinyl Chloride is available in three types, Schedule 20, 40 and 80 grade. Tinwhistle fipples usually use Schedule 40 because it is dimensionally similar to wood and Schedule 20 or 40 can be used for the tonebody. PVC drills wells, it will grab the work and chip if the drilling speeds are wrong. Can be polished but care must be taken not to burn it. Schedule 40 or 80 grade can be turned on the lathe to make sockets and tennons.

CPVC

Chlorinate Polyvinyl Chloride – This material has a yellowish color to it. It is usually slightly smaller than its equivalent PVC size. CPVC should be drilled in well-ventilated area.

ABS

Acrylnitril-Butadien-Styrol-Copolymer - usually black in color, found at many hardware stores. Molded music instruments such as recorders are usually made of. Sometimes a brown dye is used. It is a bit more durable and harder than PVC.

Delrin or Acetal

The "wonder plastic". Delrin is used very heavily for the block on Tinwhistles. It repells water in a manner that is favorable to whistle players. It can easily machined, polished if care given not to overheat. When drilling or cutting, the material usually bunches up and collects in corners. "Delrin" is the DuPont trade name, generic material is usually purchased as 'black acetal'. Note, it is also available in white.

Other Plastics
Other plastics to explore could be Acrylic, Polycarbonate, Polyethylene.

Glass
With the popular Hall Glass Flutes being made today, many have desired to use glass in whistle making. Forming fipples could proved to be difficult. Glass is extremely resonant and my recommendation is to try it for tonebodies and make the fipple out of something else.

Wood
Wood is such broad category to cover. Hardwoods should be used, possibly the very dense tropical woods in preference. Boring equipment is needed to manufacture wood whistles. Another way is to split it in half and route out the inside much like the way Native American Flutes are made.

Bamboo

Bamboo can be split in half and the nodes cleaned out to make tin whistles. Typically, the holes are made by burn through with a hot poker, a dremal tool can be used to widen the hole to desired size. It is a little difficult to predict tonehole positions since the bore the irregular. Drill all of the holes first and then gradually increase the hole diameters until the proper note is met.

Mixing different Materials

Mixing materials can have positive or negative effects on a design, many things must be taken into account. For example, a wood whistle with metal parts could have problems when the wood gets wet and swells thus causing a crack.

Plastic and metals work well together but if keys are added, remember to check the functioning at extreme temperatures, metal expands at a different rate than wood or plastic. Glass also has a certain expansion coefficient, certain metals are used with glass that have a similar expansion coefficient.

Glues

Music instrument building of the older times had few options for bonding things, shellac was employed for holding pads in place. Hide glues were used. Today we have many great options, there is contact cements and wood glues. Polyurethane glue is great for putting together headjoints. Many small parts can be bonded with CA (Cyanoacrylate glues) aka 'super glue'. Some materials like plastics do not bond well, it is recommended that when sliding on plastic pieces to be glued, small pockets and holes be cut into the material to allow glues to form 'catch pockets'. This will help prevent the pieces from separating.

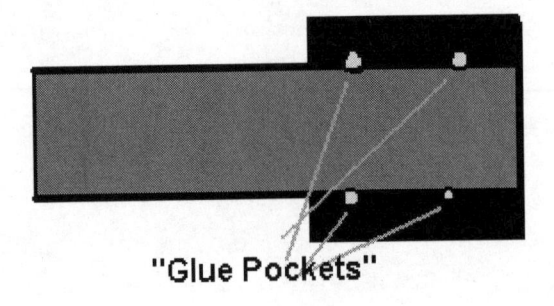

"Glue Pockets"

Alternate to glue pockets is drilling and pinning the piece.

Tools

Lathe – Needed for boring wood, making tuning couplers, turning the block.

Metal lathes are preferable for making wind instruments of any kind.

Wood lathes use various kinds gouges to cut the surface, metal lathes have a compound that moves left-to-right and various cutting bits.

If you don't have a lathe, you might be able to make some parts using a drill press.

It is desirable to find a lathe that supports boring. Boring is the process of hollowing out a piece of material. There are several ways to perform boring.

1. Wood lathe with a hollow tailstock or steady rest.

    The boring tool (drill or reamer) is inserted into a small hole in the center a slowly pushed into the work as it is turning.

2. Metal lathe with a tailstock and a drill chuck installed. The drill or reamer is inserted into the work by cranking a handle on the back of the tailstock.

3. Metal lathe with a boring mounted on the compound. This is a great way to do boring, you can adjust the position of the boring bar to bore out any side hole that you want. Longer boring bars are usually thicker, if you have to bore a long narrow hole, try to find the thickest best built boring bar possible since lengthy bore is likely to experience 'chatter' from the boring bar wobbling. Chatter is noisy, it throws off the accuracy of the cut and makes the surface very rough.

4. Gun Drills. Gun drills are special drills with motors that are mounted on the lathe and turn the opposite direction of the work being turn. This causes the bit to center on its and bore super accurately.

Bandsaw - The bandsaw makes cut pipe stock, wood, plastic a whole lot easier.

I remember when I used to cut pipe using a plumbers pipe cutter for metal whistles. It turns out that the edges of the pipe cave in on pipe cutters and this protruding into the bore deadens the volume of the instrument. When I moved up to a bandsaw, the difference was like night and day.

A decent metal hacksaw can be used for light duty work.

Drill Press – A good variable speed drill press is essential for making whistles in production. For onesy-twosey work you might be able to use a hand drill but it is very difficult to cut good holes with a hand drill. The more speeds that you have the better, having just the right speed drills smoother holes.

Hand Drill – Now that I mentioned the drill press. Hand drills can be for wire brushing the surface and other small operations. Small cordless types are best.

Dremel Tool – This little tool has many uses. In fact you can buy a light duty drill press adaptor using dremel tools. The best use for the dremel is for deburring holes. The long flexible shaft attachment double its usefulness.

Deburring Tool – A small hook shaped tool is used for deburring cut off pipe. You can get these through W.W.Grainger or Sears.

Fractional Drill Set – The sizes you have the better. It is also useful to get drills in wire gauge sizes. It will make your tonehole sizing much more accurately.

49

Cross-Vise – A vise with a cross-slide underneath. A good way for cutting windways.

See Picture:

Cross-Vise cutting windway slot using dremel cutter.

Vee-Block — A wood fixture with a 'V' shaped cutout for holding down pipe while drilling toneholes.

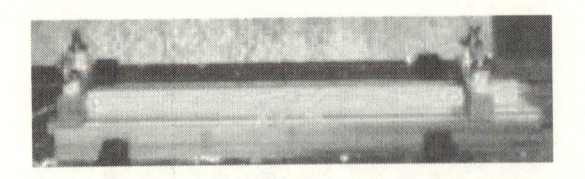

APPENDIX

Frequency Tables

Note	Freq.(Hz)	Description
C0	**16.352**	
C#0	17.324	
D0	18.354	
D#0	19.445	
E0	20.602	
F0	21.827	
F#0	23.125	
G0	24.500	
G#0	25.957	
A0	27.500	Pianos lowest note
A#0	29.135	
B0	30.868	
C1	**32.703**	
C#1	34.648	
D1	36.708	
D#1	38.891	
E1	41.203	String Bass Low E
F1	43.653	
F#1	46.249	
G1	48.999	

G#1	51.913	
A1	55.000	
A#1	58.270	
B1	61.735	
C2	**65.406**	**Organ 8' Ranks**
C#2	69.296	
D2	73.416	
D#2	77.782	
E2	82.407	Guitar Low E
F2	87.307	Contrabass Recorder
F#2	92.498	
G2	97.999	Apx. Start of Male Voice
	100 Hz	- Twice 50 Hz AC Transformer
G#2	103.826	in EU
A2	110.000	
A#2	116.541	
	120 Hz	- twice 60 Hz AC Transformer
B3	123.471	in US
C3	**130.813**	**Great Bass Recorder Organ 4'**
C#3	138.591	
D3	146.832	
D#3	155.563	
E3	164.814	
F3	174.614	Bass Recorder
F#3	184.997	
G3	195.998	
G#3	207.652	
A3	220.000	Top Bar on Bass Clef
A#3	233.082	
B3	246.942	
C4	**261.625**	**Middle C - Low-C Whistle - C Flute**
C#4	277.183	
D4	293.665	LOW-D Tin Whistle
D#4	311.127	

Note	Frequency	
E4	329.627	
F4	349.228	Alto Recorder
F#4	369.994	
G4	391.995	LOW-G Tin Whistle
G#4	415.304	
A4	440.000	A-440 Standard Pitch
A#4	466.164	
B4	493.883	
C5	**523.251**	**Soprano Recorder**
C#5	554.365	
D5	587.329	Typical Key of D Irish Tin Whistle
D#5	622.254	
E5	659.255	
F5	698.456	Sopranino Recorder Top Bar of Treble Clef
F#5	739.988	
G5	783.990	High G Tin Whistle
G#5	830.609	
A5	880.000	
A#5	932.327	
B5	987.766	
C6	**1046.502**	**Garklien Recorder**
C#6	1108.730	
D6	1174.659	
D#6	1244.507	
E6	1318.509	
F6	1396.912	
F#6	1479.977	
G6	1567.980	
G#6	1661.217	
A6	1760.000	
A#6	1864.655	Bb Clarinet Max. Pitch
B6	1975.533	
C7	**2093.004**	

C#7	2217.460	
D7	2349.317	
D#7	2489.015	
E7	2637.019	
F7	2793.824	
F#7	2959.953	
G7	3135.961	
G#7	3322.434	
A7	3520.000	Above this pitch it is difficult to identify by ear
A#7	3729.310	
B7	3951.066	
C8	**4186.008**	**Standard Piano Top Note**
C#8	4434.921	Piccolo Top Note
D8	4698.634	It doesn't really matter after this pitch
D#8	4978.029	
E8	5274.038	
F8	5587.648	
F#8	5919.906	
G8	6271.921	
G#8	6644.869	
A8	7040.000	
A#8	7458.620	
B8	7902.131	
C9	**8372.016**	
C#9	8869.841	
D9	9397.268	
D#9	9956.058	
E9	10548.075	
F9	11175.295	
F#9	11839.812	
G9	12543.843	
G#9	13289.737	
A9	14080.000	

A#9   14917.239
B9   15804.263
C10   16744.032

Note spacing is obtained by multiplying frequency by 1.059463.

Scales

Popular Major Scales

C Maj: C D E F G A B C

D Maj: D E F# G A B C# D

Eb Maj: Eb F G Ab Bb C D Eb

E Maj: E F# G# A B C# D# E

F Maj: F G A Bb C D E F

G Maj: G A B C D E F# G

A Maj: A B C# D E F# G# A

Bb Maj: Bb C D Eb F G A Bb

B Maj: B C# D# E F# G# A# B

Major Scale halftone Spacing: 2 2 1 2 2 2 1

Natural Minor Scale:

D: D E F G A Bb C D

Harmonic Minor Scale:

D: D E F G A Bb C# D

Melodic Minor Scale:

D: D E F G A B C# D

INSTRUMENT MEASURMENT TABLES

The first list of tables are for building low whistles, this covers from Low-Low-A (220Hz) to Middle-A (440Hz). The tone body sizes are adjusted for medium sized hands. The lowest pitched instruments will be a little stretch, they might require diagonal toneholes or keys if you have small hands.

BUILD SHEET

Cut the PVC pipe for the "tone body" tube to the 'Body Length' value.
Use a ruler marked in millimeters to mark off the 'pos' positions for each hole from the bottom end of the tone body. Drill the holes using the nearest drill bit sizes that correspond with 'diam' diameter.

The examples used here are for SDR21 grade PVC pipe. The size marked on the PVC is labeled ¾ inch. There is nothing on ¾" PVC tubing that is PVC. There is long explanation behind that and I think it is why plumbers make as much as they do (to keep everyone confused).

The Bore diameter is marked here as 0.910, that is a nominal inside diameter for ¾" PVC tubing.

"Tone Body length" is the value that you need to cut the body tube to.

Position of each tonehole is measured from the bottom of the tube and it is common to use millimeters for this measurement. You'll notice that wind instrument people commonly jump between Metric and English units constantly.

56

Tin Whistle Hole Spacing — Low 3/4" PVC SDR21 — Jubilee Music Instrument Co.

Note	Freq	Bore Dia	WT	Emb Width	Emb Height	Len	Hole 1 in.	Hole 2 in.	Hole 3 in.	Hole 4 in.	Hole 5 in.	Hole 6 in.	Drill 1 mm	Drill 2 mm	Drill 3 mm	Drill 4 mm	Drill 5 mm	Drill 6 mm
1 A	220.000	0.910	0.06	0.500	0.225	759	0.234	0.438	0.375	0.313	0.375	0.375	127	179	215	290	338	389
2 Bb	233.082	0.910	0.06	0.500	0.225	715	0.234	0.438	0.375	0.313	0.375	0.375	121	170	203	275	320	368
3 B	246.942	0.910	0.06	0.500	0.225	673	0.234	0.438	0.375	0.313	0.375	0.375	116	161	192	261	302	348
4 C	261.626	0.910	0.06	0.500	0.225	634	0.234	0.438	0.375	0.313	0.375	0.375	111	152	182	247	286	330
5 C#	277.183	0.910	0.06	0.500	0.225	597	0.234	0.438	0.375	0.313	0.375	0.375	106	144	173	234	270	312
> D	293.665	0.910	0.06	0.500	0.225	562	0.234	0.438	0.375	0.313	0.375	0.375	101	136	163	222	256	295
7 Eb	311.127	0.910	0.06	0.500	0.225	529	0.234	0.438	0.375	0.313	0.375	0.375	97	129	155	211	242	279
8 E	329.628	0.910	0.06	0.500	0.225	498	0.234	0.438	0.375	0.313	0.375	0.375	92	122	146	200	228	264
9 F	349.228	0.910	0.06	0.500	0.225	469	0.234	0.438	0.375	0.313	0.375	0.375	88	115	139	190	216	250
10 F#	369.994	0.910	0.06	0.500	0.225	441	0.234	0.438	0.375	0.313	0.375	0.375	84	109	131	180	204	236
11 G	391.995	0.910	0.06	0.500	0.225	415	0.234	0.438	0.375	0.313	0.375	0.375	81	103	124	171	193	224

Pennywhistle Dimensions

				15/64	7/16	3/8	5/16	3/8	3/8

SPACING

Tone Body Length		Cut Tube	Make Notch	Bottom	2	3	Top								Flute Tube	Coupl Edge	EMB Hole	Other CplEj	Block
632	1	761	721 A	2.07	1.40	1.89	2.02							767	691	710	730	742
588	2	717	677 Bb	1.91	1.32	1.76	1.91							723	647	666	686	698
546	3	675	635 B	1.77	1.25	1.64	1.81							681	605	624	644	656
507	4	636	596 C	1.63	1.19	1.53	1.72							642	566	585	605	617
470	5	599	559 C#	1.51	1.13	1.41	1.63							605	529	548	568	580
435	>	564	524 D	1.39	1.07	1.31	1.55 <							570	494	513	533	545
402	7	531	491 Eb	1.28	1.01	1.21	1.47							537	461	480	500	512
371	8	500	460 E	1.17	0.96	1.11	1.40							506	430	449	469	481
342	9	471	431 F	1.07	0.92	1.02	1.34							477	401	420	440	452
314	10	443	403 F#	0.98	0.87	0.93	1.28							449	373	392	412	424
288	11	417	377 G	0.89	0.83	0.84	1.23							423	347	366	386	398

The next set of build tables are for high whistles: This uses ½" PVC schedule 40.

Tin Whistle Hole Spacing — Low 1/2" PVC Sch 40 — Jubilee Music Instrument Co.

Not e	Freq	Bore Dia	WT	Emb Width	Emb Height	Len	Hole 1 in.	Hole 2 in.	Hole 3 in.	Hole 4 in.	Hole 5 in.	Hole 6 in.	Drill 1 mm	Drill 2 mm	Drill 3 mm	Drill 4 mm	Drill 5 mm	Drill 6 mm
1 Bb	466.164	0.622	0.109	0.375	0.225	354	0.203	0.344	0.188	0.234	0.234	0.188	66	87	119	140	169	200
2 B	493.884	0.622	0.109	0.375	0.225	333	0.203	0.344	0.188	0.234	0.234	0.188	63	82	114	133	160	190
3 C	523.251	0.622	0.109	0.375	0.225	314	0.203	0.344	0.188	0.234	0.234	0.188	60	78	108	126	152	180
4 C#	554.366	0.622	0.109	0.375	0.225	295	0.203	0.344	0.188	0.234	0.234	0.188	57	74	103	119	144	171
5 D	587.330	0.622	0.109	0.375	0.225	278	0.203	0.344	0.188	0.234	0.234	0.188	55	70	99	112	136	162
6 Eb	622.254	0.622	0.109	0.375	0.225	261	0.203	0.344	0.188	0.234	0.234	0.188	52	66	94	106	129	154
7 E	659.255	0.622	0.109	0.375	0.225	246	0.203	0.344	0.188	0.234	0.234	0.188	50	62	90	100	123	146
8 F	698.457	0.622	0.109	0.375	0.225	231	0.203	0.344	0.188	0.234	0.234	0.188	48	59	86	94	116	139
9 F#	739.989	0.622	0.109	0.375	0.225	217	0.203	0.344	0.188	0.234	0.234	0.188	46	56	82	89	110	132
10 G	783.991	0.622	0.109	0.375	0.225	204	0.203	0.344	0.188	0.234	0.234	0.188	44	52	79	84	105	126
11 A	830.610	0.622	0.109	0.375	0.225	192	0.203	0.344	0.188	0.234	0.234	0.188	42	50	75	79	99	120
							13/64	11/32	3/16	15/64	15/64	3/16						

Pennywhistle Dimensions

	Cut Tube	Make Notch	Flute Tube	Coupl Edge	EMB Hole	Other Block CpIEj
1	356	316 Bb	362	286	305	325
2	335	295 B	341	265	284	304
3	316	276 C	322	246	265	285
4	297	257 C#	303	227	246	266
5	280	240 D	286	210	229	249
^	263	223 Eb	269	193	212	232
7	248	208 F	254	178	197	217
8	233	193 F#	239	163	182	202
9	219	179 G	225	149	168	188
10	206	166 A#	212	136	155	175
11	194	154 B	200	124	143	163

SPACING

Tone Body Length	Bottom	2	3	Top
227	0.84	1.27	1.12	1.23
206	0.77	1.23	1.07	1.17
187	0.70	1.20	1.03	1.12
168	0.64	1.17	0.99	1.07
151	0.58	1.15	0.95	1.02
134 ^	0.53	1.12	0.92	0.98
119	0.48	1.10	0.89	0.94 v
104	0.43	1.08	0.87	0.90
90	0.39	1.06	0.85	0.86
77	0.35	1.04	0.83	0.83
65	0.32	1.02	0.82	0.79

Use the "Tone Body Length" to cut the tube length.

WHISTLE ASSEMBLY PICTORIAL for Low-D and other Low Whistles (Revised January 2007)

Material needed:

SDR (Schedule) 21 grade ¾" PVC (7/8" Outside diameter). About 2 or 3 foot, or more if you're making more than one, or planning to make lots of mistakes.

¾" PVC Schedule 40 coupler. Qty. 2 needed

Acetone (for cleaning).

Delrin rod stock (you can purchase from U.S Plastics or order to size from Jubilee Music

Instrument Co.) You can also use wood or other plastics in the windway but Delrin is the best.

Coping Saw or Hacksaw, pliers, Exacto knife, several small files, hook style deburring tool.

Sandpaper, (belt or disk sander optional)

Lathe (or other method of turning the delrin down to size.

Dial Calipers (or digital), you can get the dial type inexpensively at Sears.

To start, cut a piece of PVC pipe to 5 1/4 inches or 134 millimeters

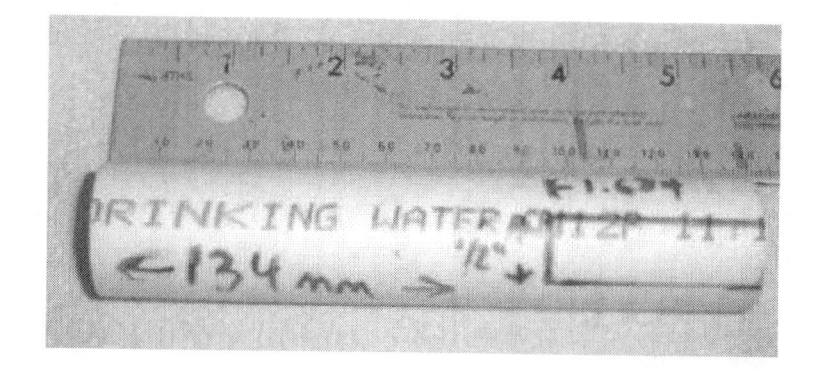

Using a marker, make a rectangular mark on the end of the pipe that is 1.634 inches deep and ½" wide.

Using a hacksaw, cut out this rectangular section.

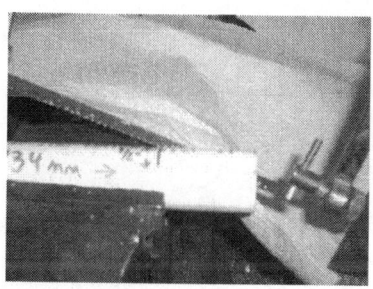

Cut carefully across as much as you can, pinching the tube with the vise will help you cut a little deeper.

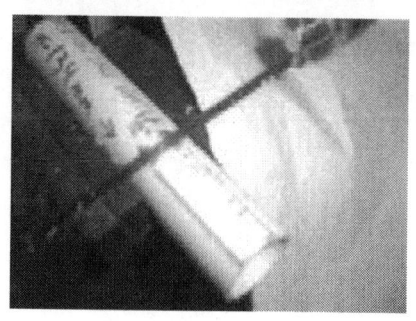

Using pliers, bend the tab downward and then upward to break off the material, over hanging material left over will be filed away.

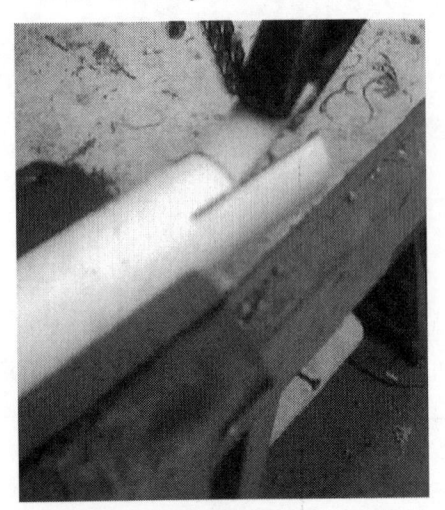

Clean up with exacto knife and file:

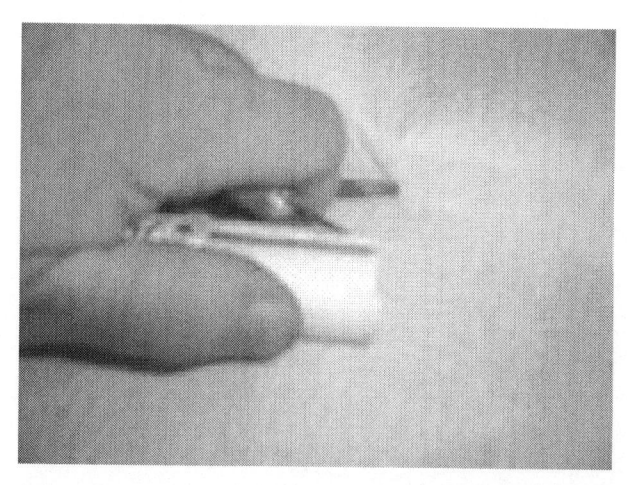

Using an Exacto knife or file, begin sliding it across with a bit of pressure to cut a ramp. Do the same on the underside, it should come to a blunt point with more material removed on top than on the bottom.

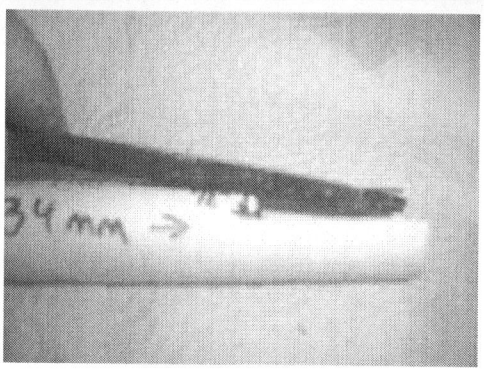

This is where most of the voicing work is done, don't rush it.

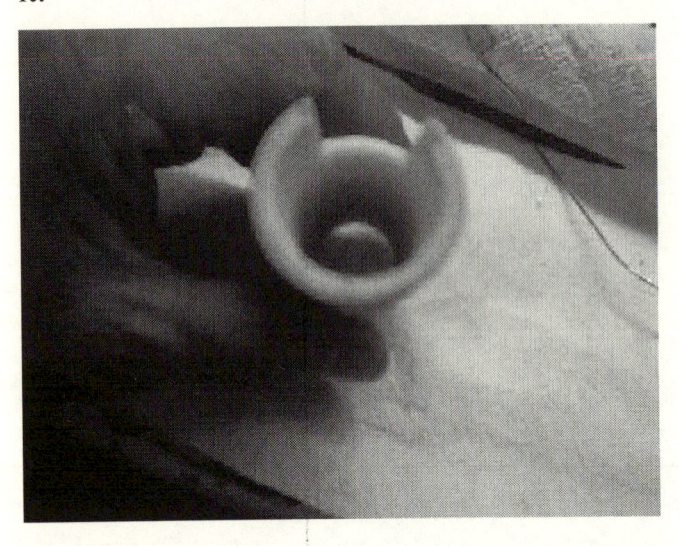

Slightly deburr the one of the PVC couplers.

Note: Couplers vary from place to place – some adjust may be in order.

Sand off any molded protrusions on the coupler, remember what side of the coupler is deburred. Also look for letters on the rim and sand those off as well so that it the finished product doesn't look like a piece of plumbing.

Sand out a section of the dividing rim inside the coupler, it should be wider than the notch that you just cut on the pipe.

File until smooth.

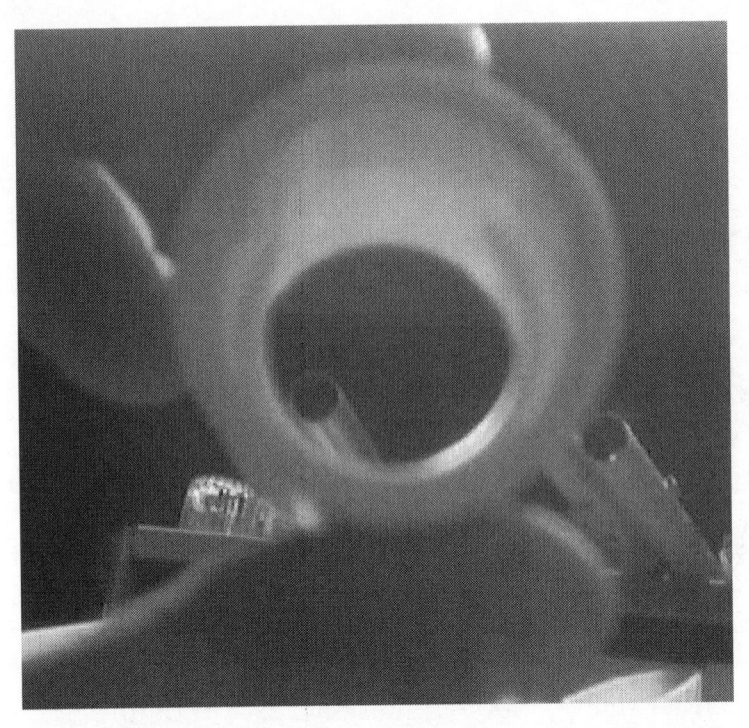

Cut out a rectangular portion on the coupler. ½" wide and 0.22 in deep.

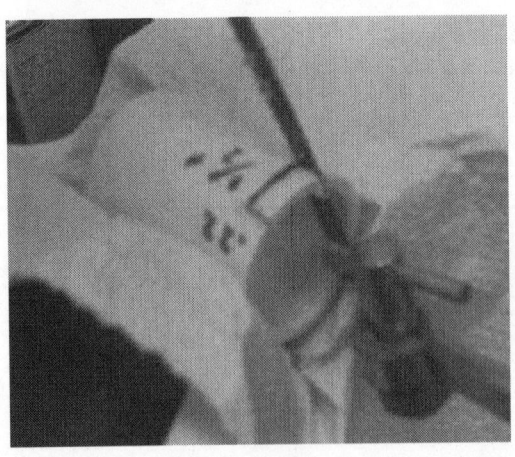

Put the coupler together to see if it lines up well with the notch.

You may notice that the windway is beginning to take shape.

Cut another piece of PVC pipe, about 2.25 inches (57 mm) long.

Put the two pieces together.

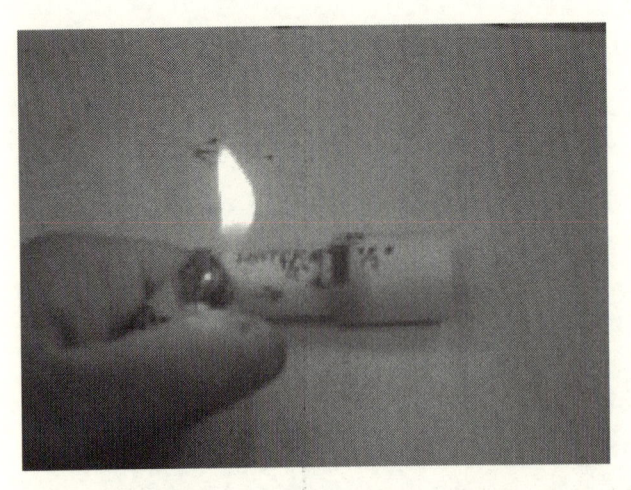

You can remove little shreds of plastic with a quick sweep of flame from a lighter.

Cut out a piece of plastic or delrin rod. (Jubilee Instruments PN: PL1)

The rod needs to be made ~0.915" in diameter and 1.634 inches long. This would require a lathe or very careful sanding and filing. Or you can purchase this from Jubilee Instruments or have made at a local shop. Alternatively, you can make this of wood – some western red cedar would work quite well.

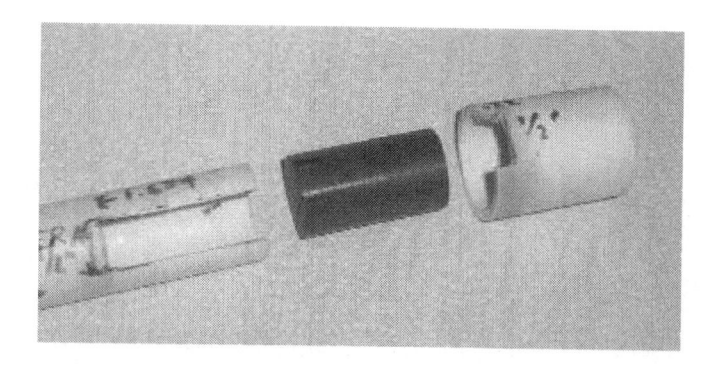

Cut out a rectangular notch on the end of the material. It should be ½" wide and 0.22 in deep.

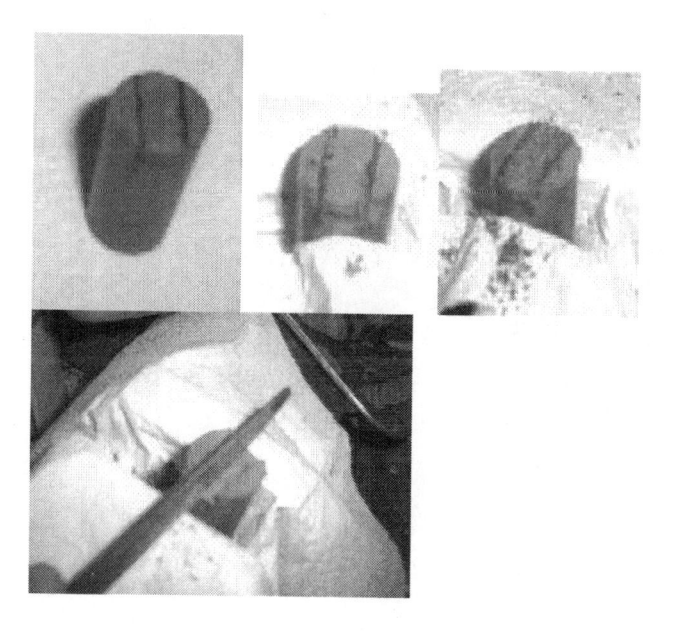

File the piece until clean and well shaped. Use a small file to chamfer the edge as well.

You may use super glue and or polyurethane glue.

Turn the block over on its underside and saw many score marks. These marks are for the glue to seep into – they will help prevent the fipple from breaking loose.

Put another coupler on the opposite end of the mouthpiece and attach a 17.125 inch piece of PVC pipe for testing.

Place the block into pipe, line it up so that the cutout area is 0.22"

Super glue along the edges (thin glue is preferable).

Also a little glue in the bottom for more strength.

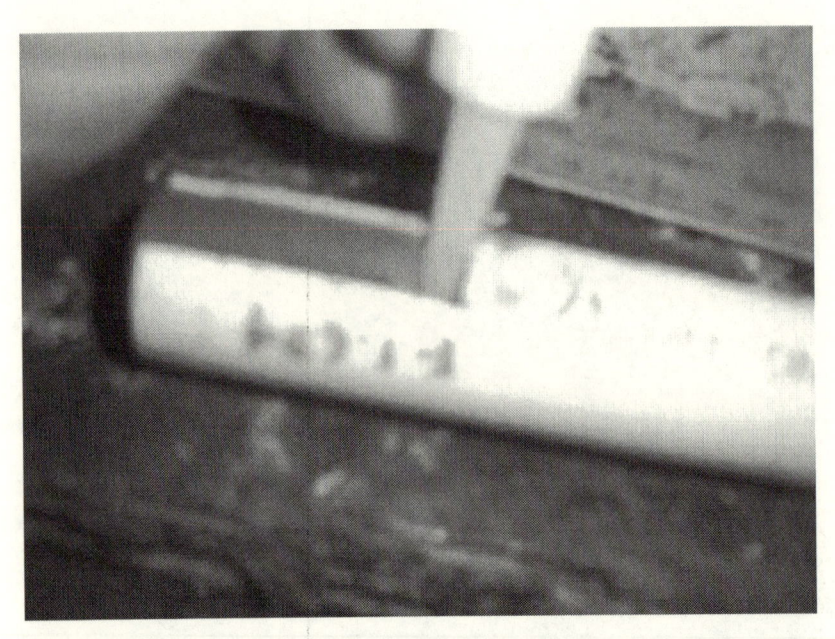

When the glue cures, you're ready to put the cover on.

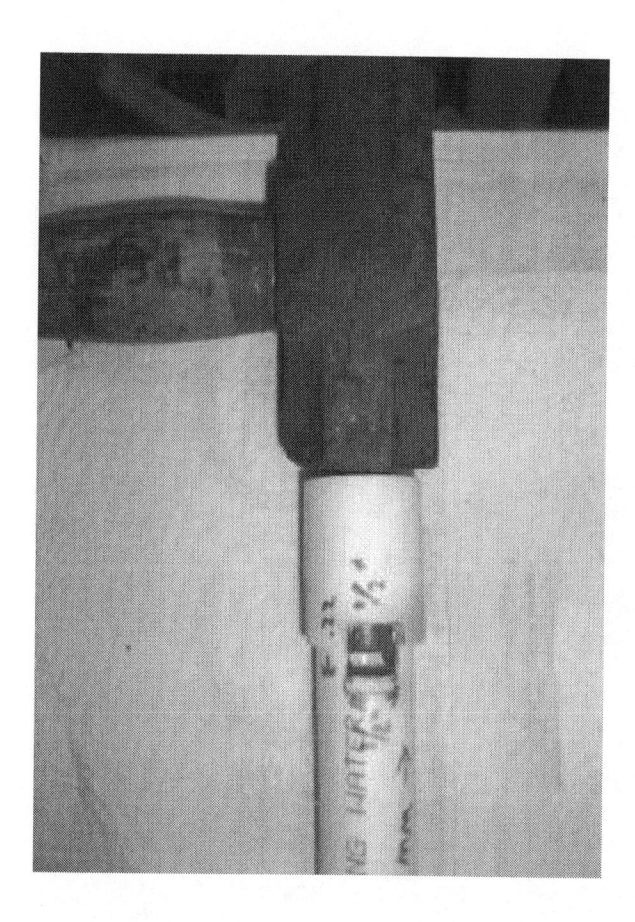

Glue the cap once it is put in place and lined up with the edge of the rod on the inside.

72

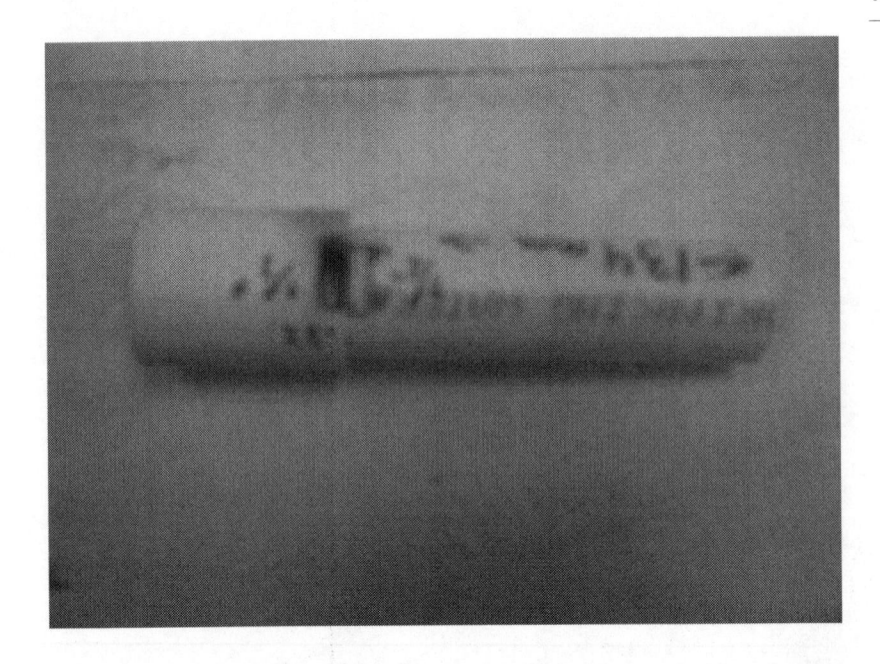

Apply a little super glue around the cap, be careful not to clog the windway with it.

A little cleanup with acetone will take the marking off of the tubing.

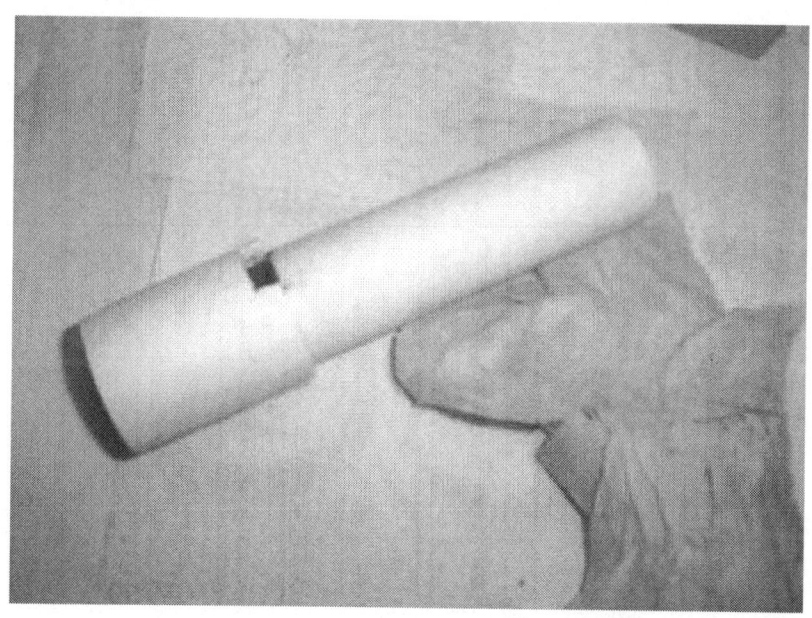

It is recommended to use latex or chemical resistant gloves when working with acetone.

Now it's time to cut the beak angle.

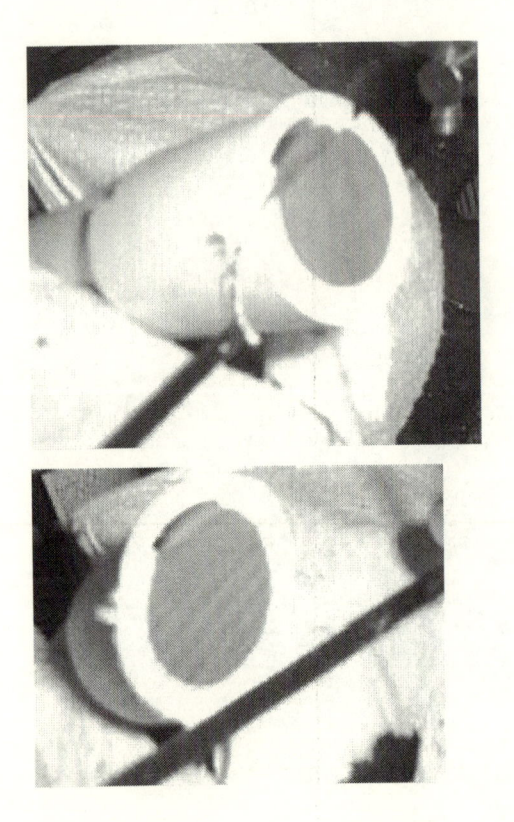

Finalize the shape with sanding:

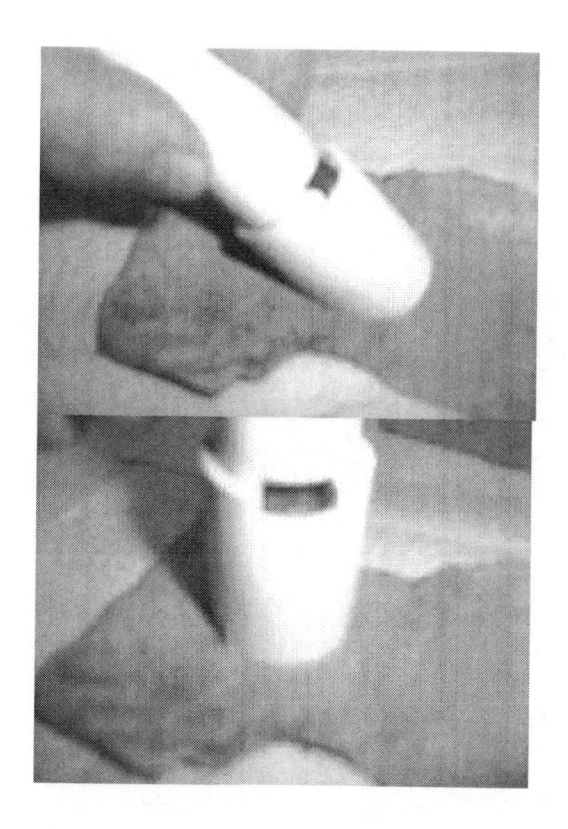

It is advised to refrain from breathing PVC sawdust, if it gets in your lungs, it will not decompose.

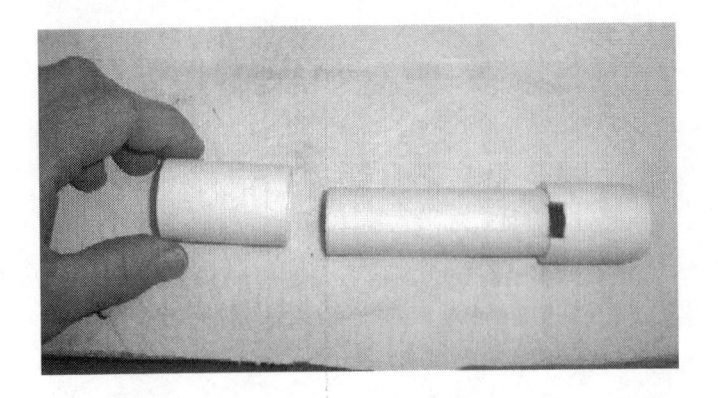

Add the plastic coupler, this serves two purposes:

1. It allows you to change tonebodies to play in different keys
2. It also serves as an adjustment for tuning.

   A completed headjoint, the bottom coupler is removable.

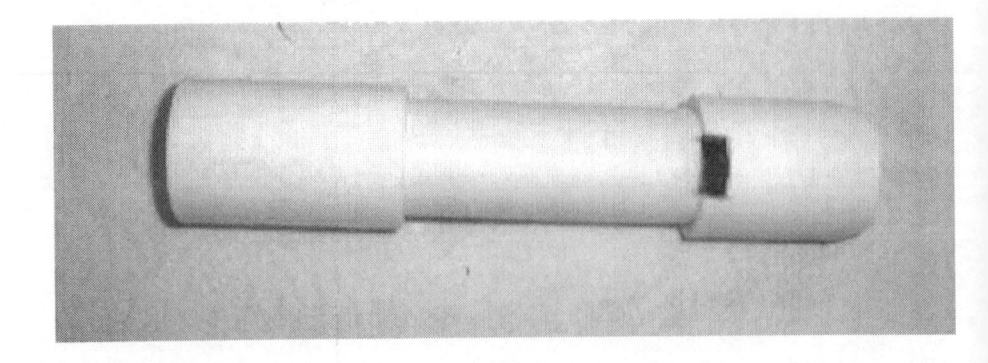

Making a PVC High Whistle.

In a manner similar to the above Low Whistle instructions, you can make a high whistle out of ½" PVC Schedule 40 PVC tubing.

Here are the measurement variations to carry out the construction of the high whistle using the same technique as the Low Whistle. Please read the Low Whistle instructions first.

2 ½ PVC couplers. The couplers I use are 1.644 inches long. Depending where you buy couplers, there could be variations that you may have to take in account for.

In this example, I cut the block from a piece of acrylic, you can still use delrin through

Turn the block to 0.622 inch diameter so that it fits snuggly inside ½" PVC tubing.

The block should be about 2-1/2 inches long. Keep it slightly long than this until your finished turning it on the lathe or whatever other method of shaping that you have used is completed. Don't forget to put the chamfer on the edge.

Profile the block so that it has a slope to the beak end of the mouthpiece

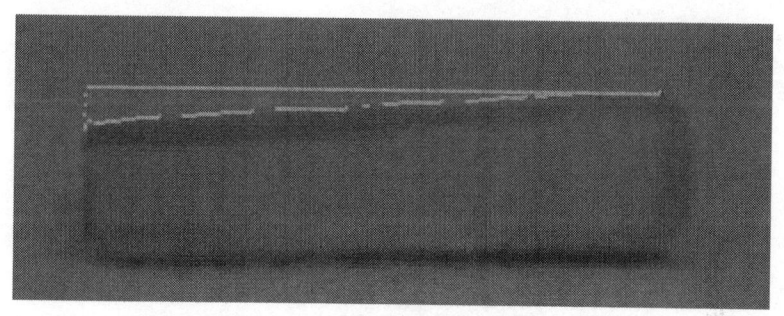

Don't profile it all of the way to the other side, leave some room for the air to straighten.

Cut a piece of ½" PVC Schedule 40 tubing for the fipple portion of the headjoint 2.23 inches long.

Cut the slot 0.855 inches long and 0.28 inches wide.

File the slot to make the fipple sharp edge just like in the Low Whistle instructions. (Gauge below reads: 2.234)

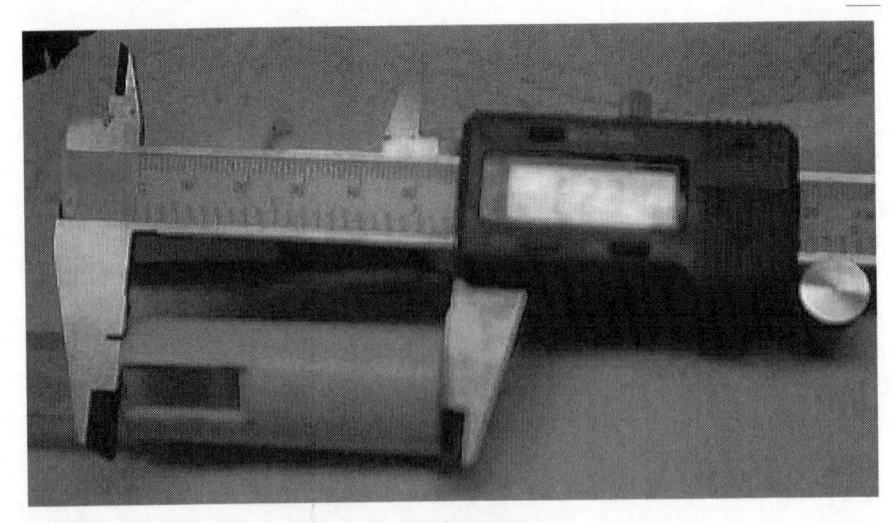

Slide the block into place, also slide the coupler into place.

Give the block and coupler about 0.221 inches from the sharp edge of the fipple window.

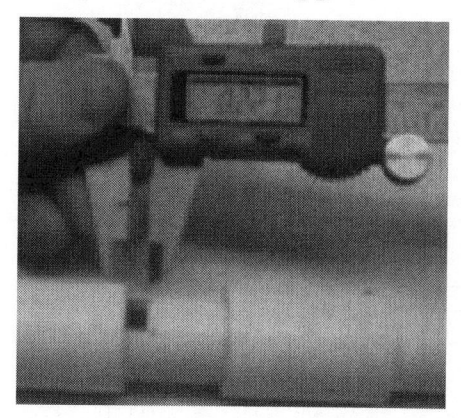

This number is not nailed in stone, you may have to adjust it to best sound.

Therefore, put the other coupler on the end of the pipe and attach a piece of PVC pipe 9.5 inches long. You can also, add a piece of PVC to fit above the fipple connector flush to the edge of the block as shown.

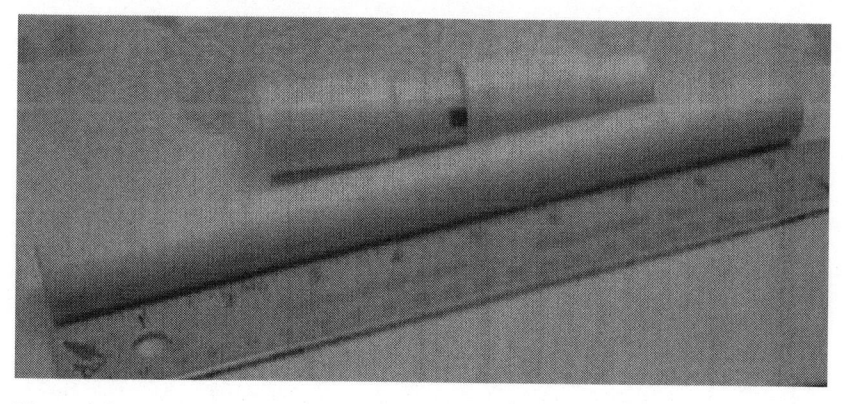

Test blow the assembly, it will produce a high C. Adjust the fipple window length for best pitch. Make sure to test at high pitch and low pitch.

When completed, seal the whole thing with a few drops of super glue on each side of the coupler and on the inside of the fipple window at the bottom of the block.

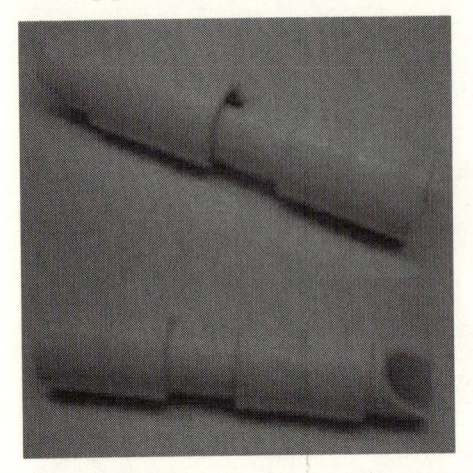

Congratulations, you have completed the fipple.

To those of you who use the metric system, be aware that ½" PVC pipe is not ½", inside diameter or outside. The original ½" goes back to the days of iron pipes, at the time the inner diameter was ½". No wonder plumbers make so much money with all the confusion.

Imagine a tin whistle made of iron pipe, a real lethal weapon!

SUPPLIERS

Ferree's Tools - Music Instrument Parts Suppliers
    Phone (616) 965-0511 WATS (800) 253-2261
    1477 E. Michigan Ave. Battle Creek, MI 49014-8950
    www.ferreestools.com

Special Shapes - Brass Tubing Supplier
    Phone (630) 759-1970 Fax (630) 759-1978
    Box 7487
    1356 Naperville Dr.
    Romeoville, IL 60446-0487
    www.specialshapes.com

K&S Metals - Tubing Supplier
    Tel (773)586-8503 Fax (773) 586-8556
    6917 West 59th Street
    Chicago, Illinois 60638
    www.ksmetals.com

Smallparts - Tubing, Delrin, etc
    Tel 1-800-220-4242 Fax 1-800-423-9009
    13980 N.W. 58th Court
    P.O. Box 4650
    Miami Lakes, FL 33014-0650
    www.smallparts.com

Copper & Brass Sales - Tubing Supplier

Tel (800) 926-2600 Fax (888) 926-2600
Multiple Locations
www.copperandbrass.com

US Plastics - Delrin Source
 1-800-809-4217   Fax 1-800-854-5498
 1390 Neubrecht Rd.
 Lima, Ohio 45801-3196
 www.usplastic.com

TAP Plastics - Delrin (Acetal) Source
 Tel 503-230-0770 Fax 503-230-1275
 2842 NE Sandy Blvd.
 Portland OR 97232
 www.tapplastics.com

Metal Supermarkets - Metal Supplier
 Tel 905-459-0466 Fax 905-459-6684
 170 Wilkinson Rd.
 Unit 18
 Brampton, Ontario, Canada
 L6T 4Z5
 Stores all over the US and Canada
 www.metalsupermarkets.com

Musictrader - Information and repair
 www.musictrader.com

Jubilee Music Instrument Co. - Parts Supplier
 Phone (513) 398-8617
 www.bingamon.com/parts.htm

I hope you have enjoyed this book, have fun building tin whistles. If you need any tin whistle building supplies mentioned in this book, contact Jubilee Music Instrument Co.

ADVERTISMENTS

The Jubilee Chromatic Whistle. Keyed Flageolet's were common in the 1800's but they began to disappear. I've ideas from the Rudal & Rose Flute system, made a few changes and developed a Chromatic Flute/Whistle The toneholes are arranged like a Low-D so that a Low-D player can take it up and start playing it immediately. Good sized toneholes allow for ornamentation of notes.

After learning the additional keys, then you can explore new capabilities in playing a tin whistle that you never had before. Every note of the octave available at your fingertips, with a 2+ octave range. The headjoint is fully compatible with the Jubilee Standard Brass Low Whistle Tonebodies so that you can use them for unusual keys.

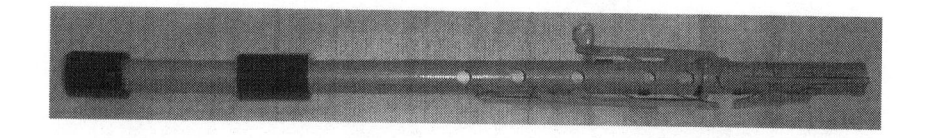

With the change of a headjoint, you can also make it a flute.

Bass Tinwhistles, one octave below Low-D.

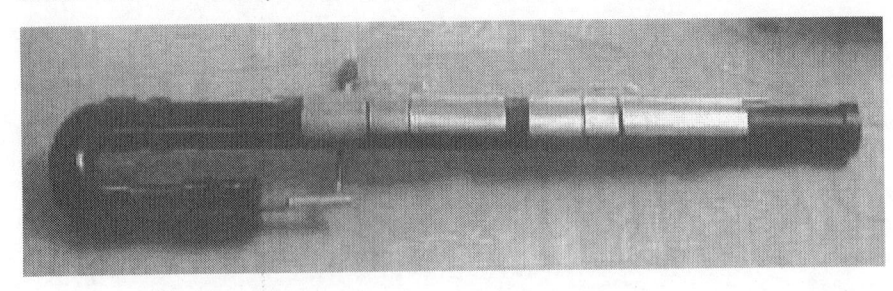

INDEX

ABS, 44

Aluminum, 8, 13, 43

Bamboo, 13, 45, 46

Bandsaw, 49

Beak, 5, 27

block, 8, 28, 40, 45, 47, 69, 79, 80, 81, 82

Bore, 5, 10, 12, 56

Brass, 8, 13, 25, 42, 43, 84, 88

Copper, 8, 13, 42, 43, 84

CPVC, 44

Cross-Vise, 50

Deburring Tool, 49

Delrin, 44, 45, 59, 84, 86

Dremel Tool, 49

Drill Press, 49

Fingering, 5, 36

Fipple Test, 5, 29

Fractional Drill, 49

Frequency, 5, 6, 11, 12, 17, 18, 19, 51

Glass, 45, 46

Hand Drill, 49

High Whistle, 14, 79

Lathe, 47, 59

Local Cutoff, 17, 18, 19

Low Whistle, 2, 14, 36, 59, 79, 80, 88

Material, 9, 42, 59

Nickel-Silver, 8, 42

Organ Ears, 31, 32

Pictorial, 6

Plastic, 46

PVC, 8, 13, 15, 23, 44, 56, 58, 59, 63, 66, 69, 76, 79, 80, 82, 83

Recorder, 7, 52, 53

Scales, 6, 55

Speed of Sound, 5, 11, 12

Stainless Steel, 8, 42

Suppliers, 6, 84

Techniques, 5, 28, 35

Tin, 1, 2, 5, 7, 8, 10, 11, 13, 18, 33, 35, 37, 39, 43, 44, 52, 53

Toneholes, 5, 14, 20

Undercutting, 5, 19

Water Trap, 31

Wavelength, 11, 12

Windsheet, 5, 27, 28, 40

Windway, 5, 27

Wood, 8, 13, 45, 48

Made in the USA
Middletown, DE
25 March 2018